GUIDANCE AND COUNSELLING

GUIDANCE AND COUNSELLING

Dr. Sunita Chhabra

GenNext Publication

ISBN : 978-93-8022-235-6

Price : 350

First Published, 2015

Published by

GenNext Publication
23, Main Ansari Road, Darya Ganj
New Delhi-110002
Ph. : 23282060, 23261060
Fax: 011-23285914
E-mail: gennext@hotmail.com

Laser Typesetting : Future Computers, Delhi
Printed at : Sagar Color Scan, Delhi

Cataloging in Publication Data—DK
Courtesy: D.K. Agencies (P) Ltd. <docinfo@dkagencies.com>

Chhabra, Sunita, author.
Guidance and counselling / Sunita Chhabra.
pages cm
ISBN 9789380222356

1. Vocational guidance—India. 2. Educational counseling—India. I. Title.

DDC 331.7020954 23

Contents

Acknowledment

Words are often too weak a mode of expression of One's deep feeling; I feel my words are not Enough to express my heartiest indebtedness to these who have assisted me in one way or the other in writing this book.

First of all, I thank the almighty for bestowing upon me the opportunities and the strength t complete this book. it is a divine grace that has lead to the successful completion of this book.

I express my gratitude to the authors and educationists whose books have been consulted. I am highly thankful to the librarian of A.C. Joshi library of Panjab University, Chandigarh for their assistance.

My Sincere thanks are to Husband (Mr. A.K. Doda) and my Ishan Doda so to express deep sense of gratitude for them for their support at every moment.

I am also grateful to gyan publishers, N. Delhi, for publishing the book.

Dr. Sunita chhabra

Date Author

Preface

Education is a vast discipline and teacher's training is a vital part of it. The responsibilities of the education and educators are focused on the task of providing better training to the future teachers for their better learning and proper development; Needless to say that this responsibility can only be exercised, if the trainers are equipped with the required knowledge of the object concerned.

A teacher is well said to be a friend, philosopher and a guide. The youth today is bewildered by the huge almost every walk of life. Life today has become so fast, the competition is cut-throat and the challenges are high. To keep pace with the ever changing demands of life, he needs to make right decisions at the right time. Not all the parents and guardians are so well equipped with the informational details and therefore this makes the role teacher even more important. The teacher can help the students in farming realistic and practical goals of life.

Here inclusion of 'Guidance and counseling' in the curriculum of teacher education programmer become very important. Every pupil teacher must have a complete and thorough knowledge of this subject and the various details of its sub-topic.

I hope, This book will develop insight into the students problem. It may stimulate teacher to provide guidance and counseling in solving the student problems.

To prepare this text book, the author consulted the works of other authors and information sources.

The author feels a deep sense of gratitude for in corporating their ideas in this book. The author is hopeful that this book would be helpful for all teachers, teacher trainees and others.

Suggestions for further modifications and improvement of the book are welcomes and will be appreciated.

Dr. Sunit chhabra

Date

Author

1

Guidance Movement in India, UK, USA

Introduction

Individuals, especially the young, face myriad problems related to growing up, social adjustment, education, and career. The guidance essential for appropriate resolution of the various crises that arise is usually provided by teachers, parents, and peer group. However, due to the complexity of modern life, the transitional nature of society, an increasing variety in the nature and extent of individual problems, trained counsellors are required for providing adequate guidance to the youth.

Guidance and Counselling is very important part of activity in educational institutions all over the world, but in India literature on this subject is very scanty. In the present book, Guidance and Counselling in India, an attempt has been made to fulfil this need in the wake of changing pattern of socio-economic, socio-educational and socio-cultural systems which are forming complex shape owing to advancement in science and technology and changing nature of human behaviour and a person's adjustment with his family, community and society.

The history of school counselling around the world varies greatly based on how different countries and local communities have chosen to provide academic, career, college readiness, and personal/ social skills and competencies to K-12 children and their families based on economic and social capital resources and public versus private educational settings in what is now called a school counselling program. In the United States, the school counselling profession began as a vocational guidance movement at the beginning of the 20th century. Jesse B. Davis is considered the first to provide a systematic school guidance program. In 1907, he became the principal of a high school and encouraged the school English teachers to use compositions and lessons to relate career interests, develop character, and avoid behavioural problems. Many others during this time did the same. For example, in 1908, Frank Parsons, "*Father of Vocational Guidance*" established the Bureau of Vocational Guidance to assist young people in making the transition from school to work. From the 1920s to the 1930s, school counselling and guidance grew because of the rise of progressive education in schools. This movement emphasised personal, social, moral development. Many schools reacted to this movement as anti-educational, saying that schools should teach only the fundamentals of education. This, combined with the economic hardship of the Great Depression, led to a decline in school counselling and guidance. In the 1940s, the US used psychologists and counsellors to select, recruit, and train military personnel. This propelled the counselling movement in schools by providing ways to test students and meet their needs. Schools accepted these military tests openly. Also, *Carl rogers'* emphasis on helping relationships during this time influenced the profession of school counselling.

Brief History of Guidance

It is very difficult to trace back the history of the origin of the guidance movement as it exists today because it has been the result of continuous efforts of individuals and institutions who from time to time have contributed to the growth of the guidance movement. Here, it is not possible to mention the names of all individuals and institutions which have contributed in the development of guidance. Only those important individuals and institutions will be referred to whose contribution has been most relevant to the movement in the present form.

As a part of the educational system in ancient India, seats of learning flourished in different regions of the country. Taxila and Nalanda

Universities were supposed to be the highest seats of learning where scholars came not only from India but also other countries i.e., China, Japan, Cambodia, Ceylon etc., to receive education at the hands of distinguished scholars. The admission to these universities was processed through a very strict admission test conducted by Dwarpandita who worked as a counsellor for the new entrants to the campus. This process of admission worked in more or less the same way as our present-day educational guidance.

In ancient India, the whole of the society was divided into four "*Varnas*" — Kshatriya, Brahmin, Vaish and Sudras. Sudras were not entitled to education. The three high castes were educated in accordance with their assigned duties. Education, in a strict sense, was only confined to Brahmins. Therefore there was hardly any question of providing guidance.

In the Muslim period, education was given in mosques and temples and was mostly of a religious nature. The mass of people remained without educational facilities. Hardly any kind of guidance was provided to the students as regards the selection of courses for study.

In British India, there was no guidance upto the end of nineteenth century except *sporadic* efforts by some individuals. The guidance movement gained impetus in the twentieth century. The development of the movement may be conveniently divided into the following two broad phases — (1.). 1900 to 1947, and (2.). 1947 to the present day.

Guidance from 1900 to 1947

As a matter of fact, the actual guidance movement was introduced in the second decade of the present century, in the year 1915. By this time psychological testing had acquired popularity in the west. In India the beginning was made by Dr G.S. Bose of Calcutta University who for the first time opened the applied psychological laboratory in the Department of Psychology of the university. *The Department of Applied Psychology* did pioneer work by using mental testing tools in India. They expenimented in providing vocational guidance on the basis of testing. No doubt, the work done in Calcutta University was not of great importance but it initiated the use of tests in guidance and has historical importance as being the first effort which generated curiosity and enthusiasm among psychologists to use tests in guidance.

The next landmark in the development of the guidance movement is the establishment of Batliboi Vocational Guidance Bureau by Mr. S.R. Batliboi in Bombay in the year 1941. The Bureau developed and standardised some aptitude tests for use in guidance. No doubt, the Bureau worked for a short period of six years but it rendered valuable service to the community and to the guidance movement since it introduced the concept of scientific guidance and aptitude testing in that city of Bombay.

The next important development was the establishment of an institution of psychological research and service in 1945 in the University of Patna. The department not only provided educational and vocational guidance to college students but also offered assistance to persons in meeting their social and personal problems. All are convinced that to tackle the personal, educational and vocational problems of our youth, guidance is necessary. State governments, universities and private agencies are doing their best to provide guidance services. The guidance services as they exist today do not cater to the needs of the masses who really need assistance in selecting educational and vocational courses. There is a great need to strengthen our guidance services to meet the demands of students.

Being encouraged by the success of the work at Patna and Calcutta, the Central Government established an employment selection bureau in the Ministry of Home Affairs and employed specialist staff.

Parsi Panchayat started a vocational guidance bureau (1947) in Bombay with the psychological tests, books and other testing materials bequeathed by Mr. Batliboi. This bureau performed excellent service to the locality of all communities by providing vocational guidance services. The bureau laid specific emphasis on counselling and individual work. Dr H.P. Mehta, its director, started the publication of a Journal Vocational and Educational Guidance. The bureau continued for more than a decade and then had to be closed due to *paucity* of funds.

The greatest landmark in the development of the guidance movement was made by the U.P. Government by establishing Bureau of

Psychology at Allahabad in 1947. The bureau spread its network throughout the state by creating district psychological centres at district headquarters. It started providing educational and vocational guidance to the students of high schools and intermediate colleges in the state. The bureau also started a diploma for graduates of psychology in *Educational Vocational Guidance.*

From 1947 to Present Day

Maharashtra and Gujarat, formerly part of the state of Bombay, started a guidance bureau in 1950 to cater to the needs of school going children. The bureau emphasised the importance of collecting and disseminating occupational information and, to train the guidance personnel to effectively manage the guidance services in schools and the community. The bureau has been making consistent efforts to create awareness about the utility of guidance among principals, teachers and parents in the state.

The *Secondary Education Commission* was appointed in the year 1952 to study the conditions of secondary education and to make recommendations for its improvement. The Commission emphasised the importance of guidance in schools. The Government of India established a Central Bureau of Educational and Vocational Guidance in 1954. The main objective of the central bureau was to coordinate the activities of state bureaus which were afterwards opened in almost all the states and to provide leadership in the field of guidance.

Keeping into consideration the importance of guidance, the All India Educational and Vocational Association was formed in 1956 to coordinate the work being done in different states. The guidance movement is gaining ground in our country. Needless to mention, there is great wastage and stagnation in our educational system right from primary to university level. The guidance services will certainly reduce the amount of wastage and stagnation.

Development of Guidance and Counselling

The need for vocational guidance has long been felt in India where, as it has been stated over and over again, there are no natural resources except human resources. The optimal use of skills and abilities has historically been identified as the best, if not only strategy to ensure national and economic development. An agency has pointed out, '*Human Capital Theory*' (now also referred to as 'Human Resource Development') has been the guiding framework for several governments, irrespective of their partisan colour or political ideology.

Vocational guidance and counselling constitutes one of the services in a range of strategies that can be used in order to 'ensure' a better fit between education and the economy, a range which includes 'man'power planning, first introduced in India at about the same time as the guidance and counselling unit of the Education Department was established. Calls for some form of vocational guidance and counselling go back at least to the turn of the century.

Clearly, the discourse and vocabulary linked to the formal field of guidance had not yet developed, but we do find expressions of concern about the lack of responsiveness of the educational sector to the needs of the labour market. As it noted in one report, hundreds of young people were 'unloaded every year by our schools', and while a minority of these did follow a University career to enter a profession, and a few others succeeded in getting a post with the government, "the bulk, whose literary and business training is most incomplete - are thrown upon a market that is already overstocked with their kind."

This chapter sets out to present a brief synthesis of the origins and development of school guidance and counselling services from 1968 to 1987. A more detailed account is available in De Giovanni (1987). In this context, it has opted to describe the main landmarks in the development of guidance — and particularly vocational guidance — providing information about the key actors promoting the field, the structures that were established in order to deliver services, and the *vicissitudes* that marked the Guidance Unit since this was set-up within the Department of Education in 1968, While emphasis will be placed on the contribution made to guidance and counselling by the Unit, it is nevertheless important to consider, albeit briefly, the activities of a large number of organisations and groups, since these generated a consensus about the need for a national guidance service, structured within and delivered through the school system.

Earlier Guidance Services

Earlier, guidance and counselling was provided informally within the context of voluntary youth organisations, non-governmental bodies and unions and the General Workers Union, and some work places (particularly in India). Within the formal education sector, individuals working for the Parents' and Students' Associations and the Education Department also declared the need for educational and vocational guidance and counselling , and organised activities in order to promote such services.

A brief word about each of these bodies and organisations, as well as a note about how their respective activities served as a catalyst in the setting up of formal guidance and counselling services, will provide the reader with a sense of the origins and development of the field in India. Given the local context, and particularly given the time-frame that is being considered, it is important to point out the extent to which religion and culture were then even more intimately intertwined than they are presently. Personal counselling was mainly a question of providing guidance and spiritual direction, while youth work was often carried out by teachers, social workers, psychiatrists, lawyers and parents worked together to offer assistance to youth through correspondence, telephone conversations and personal interviews, and a subcommittee was eventually set-up to counsel youth on issues related to vocational guidance. The latter group published pamphlets, organised lectures and courses, introduced aptitude tests, and provided a careers guidance service- another organisation, took a further step forward by organising a survey among 4000 youths in 1966. A main conclusion from this early research showed that a large number of students were leaving school without any preparation for life and that there was a felt need for vocational guidance. The social organisation urged immediate action, and there was consensus that the responsibility for providing such a service lay with the Education Department. The government recommended that officers be trained to offer a quality vocational guidance service in all schools, that guidance and counselling be introduced in the curricula of teacher training colleges, and that visits to factories and other work places should be organised to help young people become familiar with industrial settings.

Five years after the completion of the survey, a national workshop about 'Adolescent Problems in India' was organised by the government in 1959 in order to educate and prepare young engaged couples for marriage. The workshop *reiterated* the findings of the government agencies, and further alerted the public about the importance of vocational guidance for a successful insertion into the world of work.

Similar views were expressed by members of Parents' and Students' Associations, concerned as these were by the lack of guidance that students had at school, especially where this concerned career opportunities. Likewise, the teachers argued for a comprehensive guidance and counselling service for all students, and in a report which it presented in 1967, listed a number of points which it felt needed to be considered now that educational planning and secondary education for all were being placed on a solid footing. It has been noted the need for trained personnel, who would help identify the abilities and aptitudes of individual students, and guide them to appropriate educational and vocational tracks.

The movement in favour of guidance and counselling services within schools came to a head when a government agency, expert on pupil guidance assesses the real problems. The recommendations drawn up by government with in detail in a later section, given that it was instrumental in the development of guidance and counselling in schools. At this stage, it is important to point out that several organisations which have already been referred to, and which were involved in working with young people, exploited in order to make a number of proposals. The Indian government submitted a memorandum to express its concern about the lack of vocational guidance, a concern; it had been expressing from the beginning. The memorandum contained reference the importance of establishing a sound educational and vocational guidance system, led by professionally trained personnel, and to the need for stressing equality between the genders in the transition between school and work.

The government too was keen on making its set of recommendations and proposals to reintroduce its own apprenticeship scheme; closely modelling on the English system, the scheme offered technical courses of a very high quality, and registered an impressive annual success rate, attracting some of the most promising youths of the country. During discussions held with the officials pointed out that there existed a need of greater awareness in schools with regards to career opportunities. Such views reflected concerns that had long been expressed by the General Workers Union; given its awareness of the problems of young workers, and particularly so those employed in the technical sector, it had striven for the introduction of apprenticeship schemes and had stressed the need for an effective national youth employment service which would offer, among other things, a sound vocational guidance service.

While the Education Department had not established systematic guidance and counselling services in its schools prior to 1968, it had nevertheless developed a close collaboration with the Department of Labour through the services of the *Youth Employment Officer* of the time.

The Setting up of the Guidance Unit

The initiatives that have been briefly outlined in the previous section can be considered to be 'grassroots' movements in favour of guidance services for young people, articulated by different groups working at the chalk face and in different capacities with the Indian youth. Their activities, reports and proposals prepared the ground for — and led to — the establishment of a formal system of guidance and counselling within the education sector.

Terms of reference were:

(i) To review any existing educational and vocational guidance services in India.

(ii) To study the need of an organised educational and vocational guidance service, taking into consideration the recommendations of the Lewis report on educational planning.

(iii) To consider the setting up of a Guidance and Counselling Unit within the Department of Education.

(iv) To advise the Minister of Education, Culture and Tourism on the steps necessary to achieve this aim.

It also included visits to schools to hold discussions with Principals and to offer advice as to how such a unit for pupil guidance could be set up and as to what its functions were to be. It was expected to state how teachers could be trained for this purpose and what qualifications they were expected to obtain in order to become pupil guidance officers. A list of recommendations covering four key areas, namely those concerning goals and directions, those concerning the different actions that needed to be taken, those concerning administration, central bodies, and their respective duties, and those concerning the training of staff and teachers.

Initially, the Guidance Unit's main task was the creation of an infrastructure for the proper functioning of guidance in the states' education system. A scheme for the setting up of an Educational Guidance Unit within the Department of Education was finalised. The scheme was approved in toto by the Education department. The aim of the scheme was to establish guidance as an integral rather than as a peripheral activity within the education system. It was also planned that guidance and counselling services would be offered by professional personnel, who had been trained in the relevant disciplines for the purpose. The plan submitted by the newly established Guidance Unit was given full support by the Education Department.

Teacher Training

Clearly, the establishment of a Guidance Unit and the increasing attention given to guidance services within schools meant that educators, particularly teachers, had to be made aware of the nature of guidance and its hoped-for effects. In addition, the Guidance Unit required teachers in schools to be in a position to collaborate with what can be referred to as a 'guidance approach' to education. During that period, talks on guidance-related issues were organised for pupils in the Primary and Secondary Sectors in both the government and private schools. The talks were delivered by guidance officers and covered various topics including career planning and personal development.

Guidance teachers were to be assigned a reduced teaching load equivalent to half the normal load, so that they could dedicate the other half to guidance duties. The complement of guidance teachers was to be regulated by the ratio of pupils.

Conclusion

The Guidance and Counselling Unit developed several important services. In the space of almost fifty years, it had built up a team of qualified staff whose duties included:

(i) Regular guidance and counselling sessions in schools;
(ii) Counselling individual students referred by Heads of Schools;
(iii) Organising talks and seminars for school-leavers;
(iv) Preparing career orientation conventions;
(v) Collecting information about different careers, and passing on this information to interested students;
(vi) Providing information and guidance regarding educational opportunities;
(vii) Supporting the Heads of schools in the exercise of streaming, and student choice of optional courses;
(viii) Organising orientation visits to institutions of higher and further education, industries and other work places;
(ix) Meeting parents in order to facilitate understanding of school policy regarding subject option choices;
(x) Liaising with other government departments and helping agencies (including the Department of Labour, the Department of Social Welfare, the Youth Service Organisation, the Forensic Department, the Special Education Section, the **Health Education Unit,** the **Child Guidance Clinic,** the Youth Employment Service and **Caritas.**

On the basis of such achievements, the Guidance and Counselling Services could look forward to increased commitment to the needs of students, in response to changes in the educational system, in social mores and values, and in the structure of opportunities in employment market.

In the Context of India

The articles published in media presents a report on the contribution made by India in the field of counselling . India has had a long history of educational development presenting many marked contrasts to American education. Guidance in India has existed for some years and is progressing, but there are numerous problems which tend to hinder development. Educational and vocational guidance in the schools will be pushed in the Third Five-Year Plan, but first the youngsters and young people must be placed in the schools. Another complication in the educational picture is the fact that only about half of the students who have completed high school are able to pass the school-leaving examination successfully and so receive their certificates. Before examining the changes in the educational program and the progress of the guidance movement, several other problems should be briefly mentioned. India's history is ancient and amazingly complex. Only in the past thirteen years has there been political unity and freedom from outside domination. The government and the people are busy at the tremendous task of trying to hurdle the centuries and to attain economic and industrial sufficiency. India has moved ahead in the field of guidance but there are many obstacles to overcome. The size of the tasks to be accomplished is almost overwhelming.

History of Guidance in USA

Early years: In the United States, the school counselling profession began as a vocational guidance movement at the beginning of the twentieth century. *Jesse B. Davis* is considered the first to provide a systematic school guidance program. In 1907, he became the Principal of a high school and encouraged the school English teachers to use compositions and lessons to relate career interests, develop character, and avoid behavioral problems. Many others during this time did the same. For example, in 1908, *Frank Parsons,* "Father of Vocational Guidance" established the Bureau of Vocational Guidance to assist young people in making the transition from school to work.

From the 1920s to the 1930s, school counselling and guidance grew because of the rise of progressive education in schools. This movement emphasized personal, social, moral development. Many schools reacted to this movement as anti-educational, saying that schools should teach only the fundamentals of education. This, combined with the economic hardship of the Great Depression, led to a decline in school counselling and guidance.

In the 1940s, the US used psychologists and counsellors to select, recruit, and train military personnel. This propelled the counselling movement in schools by providing ways to test students and meet their needs. Schools accepted these military tests openly. Also, *Carl Rogers'* emphasis on helping relationships during this time influenced the profession of school counseling.

1950s and 60s: In the 1950s the government established the Guidance and Personnel Services Section in the Division of State and Local School Systems. In 1957, the Soviet Union launched Sputnik. Out of concern that the Russians were beating the US in the space race, which had military implications, and that there were not enough scientists and mathematicians, the American government passed the *National Defense Education Act,* which spurred a huge growth in vocational guidance through large amounts of funding. Since the 1960s, the profession of school counselling has continued to grow as new legislation and new professional developments were established to refine and further the profession and improve education.

On January 1, 2006, congress officially declared February 6–10 as National School Counselling Week.

The 1960s was also a time of great federal funding in the United States for land grant colleges and universities interested in establishing and growing what are now known as Counselor Education programs. School counselling began to shift from a focus exclusively on career development to a focus on student personal and social issues paralleling the rise of social justice and civil rights movements in the United States. It was also in the late 60s and early 1970s that Norm Gysbers began the work to shift from seeing school counsellors as solitary professionals into a more strategic and systemic goal of having a comprehensive developmental school counselling program for all students K-12. His and his colleagues' work and research evidence showing strong correlations between fully implemented school counselling programs and student academic success was critical to begin to show an evidence base for the profession especially at the high school level based on their work in the state of Missouri.

1980s and 90s: But school counselling in the 1980s and early 1990s in the United States was not seen as a player in educational reform efforts buffeting the educational community. The danger was the profession becoming irrelevant as the standards-based educational movement gained strength in the 1990s with little evidence of systemic effectiveness for school counselors. In response, *Campbell and Dahir (1997),* consulted widely with school counselors at the elementary, middle, and high school levels and created the ASCA National Standards for School Counselling with three core domains (Academic, Career, Personal/Social), nine standards, and specific competencies and indicators for K-12 students.

The publication of the ASCA standards in 1997 ushered in a unique period of professionalization and strengthening of school counselling identity, roles, and programs. A year later, the first systemic meta-analysis of school counselling was published and gave the profession a wake-up call in terms of the need to focus on outcome research and the small set of methodologically accurate school counselling outcome research studies in academic, career, and personal/social domains.

National Center for Transforming School Counselling : Also in the late 1990s, a former mathematics teacher, school counselor, and administrator, *Pat Martin,* was hired by The Education Trust to work on a project focussing the school counseling profession on helping close achievement gaps hindering the life successes of children and adolescents, including children and adolescents of colour, poor and working class children and adolescents, bilingual children and adolescents and children and adolescents with disabilities.

Martin's project developed focus groups of K-12 students, parents, guardians, teachers, building leaders, and superintendents and interviewed professors of school counselling in Counsellor Education programs. She hired a school counsellor educator from Oregon State University, Dr Reese House, and they co-created what became the National Center for Transforming School Counselling at The Education Trust in 2003.

Their foci included (*1*) changing how school counselling was taught at the graduate level in Counselor Education programs and (*2*) changing the practices of K-12 school counselors in districts throughout the USA to teach school counselors prevention and intervention skills to help close achievement and opportunity gaps for all students. The NCTSC focus groups found what *Hart & Jacobi (1992),* had indicated—too many school counselors were working as gatekeepers for the status quo instead of advocates for equity. Too many school counselors were using inequitable practices and unwilling to challenge them, which kept students from nondominant backgrounds from the advanced coursework (honours, AP, IB courses) and academic, career, and college readiness skills needed to successfully graduate from high school and pursue rigorous post-secondary options including college.

They found funding for $500,000 grants for six different Counsellor Education/School Counselling programs in rural and urban settings, to transform their School Counselor Education programs to focus teaching school counselor candidates advocacy, leadership, teaming and collaboration, equity assessment using data, and culturally competent program counselling and co-ordination beginning in 1998 (Indiana State University, University of Georgia, University of West Georgia, California State University - Northridge, University of North Florida, and Ohio State University) http://www.edtrust.org/node/139 and then over 25 other Counsellor Education/School Counselling programs joined as companion institutions in the following decade. By 2008, NCTSC consultants had also worked in over 100 districts around the United States including most major cities to help transform the work of school counselors to help close gaps and challenge in appropriate policies and procedures through the use of data and assessing equity. Practitioners, too, jumped on board the school counselling transformation train. In 2008, Rowman Little field Education published.

The New School Counsellor: Strategies for Universal Academic Achievement. The text, written by *Rita Schellenberg,* a practising school counsellor and counselor educator, describes the new vision for school counselling and guides school counsellors and pre-service school counsellors through accountable, data-driven programming. Schellenberg introduces Standards Blending, a cross-walking strategy that hold the potential to be culturally sensitive and effective in enhancing academic achievement and closing the achievement gap.

> ***Recent history:*** In 2002, the American School Counsellor Association released the ASCA National Model framework for school counselling programs, written by *Dr Trish Hatch* and *Dr Judy Bowers,* comprising some of the top school counselling components in the field into one model—the work of Norm Gysbers, Curly and Sharon Johnson, Robert Myrick, Dahir and Campbell's ASCA National Standards, and the skill-based focus for closing gaps from the Education Trust's Pat Martin and Reese House into one document. ASCA also developed the RAMP (Recognised ASCA Model Programs) Awards to honor school counselling programs that have fully implemented the ASCA National Model with demonstrable evidence of success for K-12 students.

In 2003, the Center for School Counselling Outcome Research was developed as a clearing house for evidence-based practice with regular research briefs disseminated and original research projects developed and implemented with founding director *Jay Carey.* One of the research fellows, *Tim Poynton,* developed the EZ Analyse software program for all school counselors to use as free-ware to assist in using data-based interventions.

In 2004, the ASCA Code of Ethics was substantially revised to focus on issues of equity, closing gaps, and ensuring all students received access to a K-12 school counselling program. Pat Martin left the Education Trust and moved to the College Board. She hired School Counselor Educator *Dr Vivian Lee* and they developed an equity-focused entity on school counselors and college counseling, the National Office for School Counselor Advocacy (NOSCA). NOSCA developed scholarships for research on college counselling by K-12 school counselors and how it is taught in School Counselor Education programs. They also created Advocacy Awards to focus on best practices in college counselling programs in K-12 schools that show effective school counselling practices in creating college-going cultures with demonstrated results in ensuring high rates of college admissions for large percentages of students of nondominant backgrounds.

In 2008, the first NOSCA study was released by Jay Carey and colleagues focusing on innovations in selected College Board "Inspiration Award" schools where school counselors collaborated inside and outside their schools for high college-going rates and strong college-going cultures in schools with large numbers of students of nondominant backgrounds. Also in 2008, the American School Counselor Association released School Counselling Competencies focused on assisting school counselling programs to effectively implement school counselling programs based on the ASCA Model.

The ASCA Model encourages professional school counselors to use crosswalking strategies and to create action plans and results report that demonstrate "how" school counselors are making a difference in the lives of students. In 2008, *Dr Rita Schellenberg* introduced Standards blending as a crosswalking strategy to aid in aligning school counselling more directly with the academic achievement mission of schools. Scholars have identified Standards Blending as a promising approach for enhancing academic achievement and closing the achievement gap. At the same time, Dr. Schellenberg introduced the School Counselling Operational Plan for Effectiveness (SCOPE) and the School Counselling Operational Report of Effectiveness (SCORE), a data reporting system to demonstrate accountability practices and program outcomes. The SCOPE and SCORE are designed to simplify the task of creating action plans and results reports with immediate access to the ASCA and core academic standards, data sources, and data analysis tools. The most recent version of the ASCA National Model was published in 2012.

The history of the profession continues shifting as more students, parents, guardians, teachers, building leaders, and government officials learn of changes in the profession, and as the evidence base and equity-building skills of school counselor candidates and school counselors in K-12 schools develop through the dissemination of results and successful outcomes of increased student academic, career, college, and personal/social competencies including reduced achievement and opportunity gaps for all students.

Other Countries: A balanced, comprehensive school counselling program provides services to promote student success. It involves school counselors working in conjunction with parents, teachers and other school personnel and community agencies. Many developmental concepts that must be covered through a comprehensive program can be incorporated into other classroom studies, giving the school counselor more opportunities for direct counseling, prevention, and remediation functions. It is important that a comprehensive school counselling program provide a range of services in order to address the needs of all students. Counselors should strive to balance their time among all these services, based on the unique needs of their school community. By developing and implementing a comprehensive school counselling plan, school counselors can establish services and activities that allow them to spend most of their time providing direct services to children.

In the United States, the school counselling profession began as a vocational guidance movement at the beginning of the twentieth century (Schmidt, 2003, p. 6). In 1907, Jesse B. Davis became the Principal of a high school and encouraged the school English teachers to use compositions and lessons to relate career interests, develop character, and avoid behavioral problems. From that grew systematic guidance programs which later evolved into comprehensive school counselling programs that address three basic domains: academic development, career development, and personal/social development.

2

Guidance

Introduction

We are social beings and, so in some way or other we need help and guidance of others. Mother, father, grand parents, and teachers and other elders, home, school and society guide youngsters for successful living. Due to explosion of knowledge, industrialisation and changes in socio-economic set-up the need of professional guidance is felt in the present day society.

It is a truism that a very minor percentage of our total population is capable of handling its problems independently without the cooperation and guidance of others. We find that majority of the people do not have either confidence or insight to solve their problems. They seek advice or guidance from others wherever there is a problem. There have always been people in the past who need occasional help from older or more experienced associates in meeting with their problems of daily life in the society.

Traditionally, in our Indian society, the leader of the family or the local community was supposed to provide the necessary guidance and advice whenever it was needed by any member of the family or the community. Needless to mention too often informal advice, given without a clear understanding of the problem involved, was likely to be not only ineffectful but harmful and misleading to the individual. With the passage of time, revolutionary changes have taken place in the fields of medicine, industry, business and agriculture etc. Changes in all walks of life coupled with extraordinary growth in our population have made the social structure very complex. The varieties of jobs, aspirations of multitudes for jobs, and minute vocational specialization have made the work of guidance very difficult. The head of the family or leader of the local community with his limited knowledge of the changed conditions is not capable of providing guidance to the youth of today. In the last four decades, guidance movement has spread like a wildfire throughout the world and has generated a great amount of enthusiasm and zeal among parents, teachers and social workers who have devoted time to explore its feasibility and utility for the general population including school-going adolescents. All are convinced that proper provision of guidance services should be made for children at different age levels for the harmonious development of their personalities in the larger interest of the society and the individuals.

In this unit you will be familiarised with concept, principles, need of guidance and implications of areas of guidance on global context.

Meaning of Guidance

Literally guidance means to direct, to point out, and to show the path. It is the assistance or help rendered by a more experienced person to a less experiences person to solve certain major problems of the individual (less experienced) i.e., educational, vocational, personal etc. Guidance is a concept as well as a process. As a concept guidance is concerned with the optimal development of the individual. As a process guidance helps the individual in self- understanding (understanding one's strengths, limitations, and other resources) and in self-direction (ability to solve problems, make choices and decision on one's own).

Guidance is a concept as well as a process. Guidance is different from education and counselling. Guidance is based upon the principles of holistic development of individual, recognition of individual differences and dignity and acceptance of individual needs. Guidance is needed wherever there are problems. Guidance helps in optimum development of individual, solving different problem of the individual, Academic growth and development, Vocational maturity, vocational choices and vocational adjustments, Social personal adjustment. Better family life, for conservation and proper utilization of human resources, and national development. Guidance is helpful not only for student and teacher in an educational institution but also to the parents, administrators, planners and community members. A school guidance programme includes all those activities other than instructional which are carried out to render assistance to pupils in their educational, vocational, personal development and adjustment. The areas of guidance are very vast. Some of the important areas of guidance are personal, educational, vocational, avocational, health, social etc.

Guidance, in India, is comparatively a new field within the larger and more inclusive field of education. It covers the whole spectrum of education which starts from the birth of the child and continues till his death. This is a wide meaning of the term which includes all types of educaiton, formal, nonformal, vocational etc., which aims to adjust the individual in his environment in an effective way. Another meaning of the term is that guidance is a specialized service whose primary concern is with the individual. It may be said that guidance is given to individuals in making intelligent choice and adjustments. It is based on the democratic principle that it is the duty and right of every individual to choose his own way in life insofar as his choice does not interfere with the rights of others.

D.G. Mortensen: et al, in their book Guidance in Today's Schools have defined guidance as "That part of the total educational programme that helps provide the personal opportunities and specialized staff services by which each individual can develop to the fullest his abilities and capacities in terms of the democratic ideal."

According to the *National Vocational Guidance Association* (NVGA), "Guidance is the process of helping a person to develop and accept an integrated and adequate picture of himself and of his role in the world of work, to test this concept against reality and to convert it into reality with satisfaction to him and benefit to society."

Welty, Turral and Weitzel say that "Guidance is that systematic, organised phase of the educational process which helps youth grow in his power to give point and direction to his own life, to the end that he may gain richer personal experiences while making his unique contribution to our democratic society."

Guidance, as defined by *Jones,* "Guidance is the help given by one person to another in making choices and adjustments and in solving problems."

Guidance and Education: The aim of education is to achieve the fullest possible realization of possibilities inherent in the individual. Education fosters all aspects of an individual's personality. Guidance is an integral part of education and helps in achieving the goals of education. Guidance is quite essential for the development of individual which is the main objective of education. *The Education Commission (EC-1964–66)* observes Guidance should be regarded as an integral part of education and not as a special, psychological or social service which is *peripheral* to educational purposes. It is meant for all students not just for those who deviate from the norm in one direction or the other.

Jone, A.J., pointing out the relationship between guidance and education observes—all guidance is education but some aspects of education are not guidance. Their objectives are the same the development of the individual but methods used in education are by no means the same as those used in guidance.

Guidance and Counselling: The terms guidance and counselling have been loosely or inter-changeably used. Guidance is a term which is broader than counselling and it includes counselling as one of its services. Butter makes a logical separation of the counselling process i.e., (*a*) adjustive and (*b*) distributive phase. In the adjustive phase, the emphasis is on social, personal and emotional problems of the individual, in the distributive phase the focus is upon educational, vocational and occupational problems. The distributive phase can be most aptly described as guidance while the adjustive phase can be considered as description of counselling.

Principles of Guidance

Guidance is based upon the following principles:

(i) ***Holistic development of individual:*** Guidance needs to be provided in the context of total development of personality.

(ii) ***Recognition of individual differences and dignity:*** Each individual is different from every other individual. Each individual is the combination of characteristics which provides uniqueness to each person. Similarly, human beings have an immense potential. The dignity of the individual is supreme.

(iii) ***Acceptance of individual needs:*** Guidance is based upon individual needs i.e., freedom, respect, dignity.

(iv) ***The individual needs*** a continuous guidance process from early childhood throughout adulthood.

(v) Guidance involves using skills to communicate love, regard, respect for others.

Need and Importance of Guidance

The basic question which may be asked here is — What is the need for guidance? Why should it be given to an individual? Man when born is not capable of independent working. He is born with certain biological inheritance which does not render him capable of adjustment in his physical environment. The human child remains dependent for the longest period on his parents who are responsible for his development in early childhood.

Human beings by nature tend to seek advice and assistance from others whenever they are confronted with a problem. It is assumed that a person is bound to seek assistance from others, and the advice or assistance which other persons provide may not-always be of great use or may some time prove harmful. Then why should guidance not be provided in a properly organized and systematic way? So there is a great need to provide necessary guidance at the appropriate time by well-qualified personnel.

India is a democratic country. Education which was confined to classes has now reached the masses with the declaration of univeralization of education and equal educational opportunities to all irrespective of caste, colour, region, economic and social difference. The success of democracy depends on educated and enlightened individuals who should share the responsibilities of running the administration smoothly and efficiently.

Guidance is an integral part of Education. Guidance is necessary for the following reasons:

(*a*) Guidance services if properly organised help to eliminate wastage and stagnation by developing the curriculum according to the needs and abilities of students.
(*b*) Students are helped to select courses according to their abilities, interests and aptitudes.
(*c*) Guidance services decrease the number of misfits by helping such cases to see things realistically and adjust themselves.
(*d*) Students are prepared for professional leadership in the changed socio-economic and industrial conditions in which different occupations have emerged which require specialized training.
(*e*) The child's healthy growth is encouraged.
(*f*) Problems of discipline and delinquency are solved.
(*g*) It helps to supply the right personnel for various jobs in private and public sectors.
(*h*) The population in our country is increasing at a tremendous rate and if it is not checked it will create chaotic conditions in the country. The individuals require guidance to plan their family.
(*i*) The increase in population, industrialization and westernization have created a number of problems for our adolescents who are facing frustration, conflicts and tensions and other strain and stress in the present decade. It is imperative to provide guidance to the young generation to save them from stress and strain of a developing society.
(*j*) Individuals differ in physical, mental, social and emotional characteristics. To provide for the maximum development of individuality, guidance is essentially needed, particularly for exceptional children.
(*k*) Problems of women are emerging as a new area where guidance is needed for proper adjustment in the family. The cases of divorce, separation and desertion are very rapidly increasing in our society which are posing a new threat to our traditional social system.
(*l*) There are other problems which are unique to our society as for instance problems of scheduled castes, problems of social conflicts, problems of retired persons and problems of industrial relations where guidance is needed.

Functions of Guidance

Guidance as interpreted by workers in the field is applicable to all aspects of human life, i.e. physical, mental, social and emotional in all stages of development right from infancy to old age. The main objective of guidance is to help the individual to utilize his basic potentialities to the maximum for adequate adjustment in the environment. The following specific and interrelated functions are common to all types of guidance services:

(*a*). The first function of guidance is to understand the individual and discover the real needs and problems of individuals and to explore the possibilities of personality development within the context of the education process.

(*b*). The second function is to use information collected about students to adjust, instruction to meet individual needs and to help to develop attitudes and patterns of behaviour that can help each individual to develop optimally.

(*c*). The third function is to develop among teachers a greater understanding of child growth and development.

(*d*). The fourth function is to provide such specialized services as orientation, individual inventory, counselling, occupational information, group guidance, placement and follow-up services.

(*e*). The last and important function is to provide information and feedback conditioning research which evaluates the success of the programme of guidance of various types. The results of research, testing and related studies about young people must be supplied on a continuing basis to administrators, curriculum planners and teachers as a means of ensuring the proper climate and conditions for learning.

Scope of Guidance Services

Guidance is not a once-for-all activity but is a continuous process in the life of the individual. The following are the specific activities which fall within the purview of guidance:

(a) **Personal** : Social problems of the individual, their diagnosis and prescribing remedial measures to resolve them.

(b) Educational problems of the individual, and to suggest remedial measures for their resolution.
(c) **Vocational problems** : Helping the individual in the choice of an appropriate vocation and aiding him to acquire proficiency in the vocation.
(d) **Appraisal of individuals** : Students' appraisal is an important aspect of guidance personnel's work, which helps students to develop their potentialities to the maximum.
(e) **Counselling** : After making appraisal through various test and non-test techniques the guidance worker provides counselling to the counsellee keeping into consideration the strengths and weaknesses of his personality and other variables operating in the environment.
(f) **Placement** : In the placement services the counsellee is placed in an appropriate course vocation on the basis of guidance provided to him.
(g) **Follow-up and Research** : Follow-up is a process in which the guidance personnel follow up the *incumbents* after placing them in a course vocation and see whether they are progressing satisfactorily. Research is also one of the important activities in guidance through which curricular programmes are modified and improved.

Guidance and its Relationships

Guidance as a helping profession is closely related to all subjects and disciplines which are directly concerned with human beings and their welfare, for instance, education, humanities, sciences, discipline, administration and curriculum. Here we will discuss the relationship of guidance to education, curriculum and discipline only.

Different School Guidance Services

The school is expected to provide more than just teaching and instruction. A school guidance programme includes all those activities other than instructional which are carried out to render assistance to pupils in their educational, vocational, personal development and adjustment. The fundamental aim of guidance programme being the maximum development of the child, all guidance programmes must be geared toward attainment of the goal. Guidance services can assist the pupils in knowing themselves-their potentialities and limitations, making appropriate choices in educational, vocational and other fields. Some of the important guidance services are;

(i) The orientation services
(ii) Student Inventory services
(iii) Career Informations services
(iv) Counselling services
(v) Group guidance services
(vi) Placement services
(vii) Research and evaluation services

Implications of Areas of Guidance in Global Context

The students' life is getting complex day by day. Students in the twenty-first century have facing many perplex and difficult situations i.e., to make wise curricular and other curricular choices, to acquire basic study skills for optimum achievement, adjustment with peers etc. In its beginning guidance was concentrated on problems relating to vocations. It was largely concerned with getting jobs for young people. Now guidance has gone for beyond this. It is now concerned with the entire individual in all aspects. The areas of guidance are very vast. The following are some of the important areas of guidance:

Personal: Students face many personal problems related to themselves, their parents and family, friends and teachers, etc. They often have memories related to home or family which creates feeling of disappointment in them. If their parents are expecting too much of them it leaves them with a feeling of incompetence and insecurity leading poor self-concept and self esteem. The objectives of personal guidance are to help the individual in his/her physical, emotional, social, rural and spiritual development. The aims and objectives of personal guidance are:

(i) To assist the individual in understanding himself/herself.
(ii) To assist the individual involving the personal problems.

(iii) To assist the individual in taking independent decisions and judgement.
(vi) To assist the individual to view the world and the social environment in right perspective.
(v) To assist the individual in making sound adjustments to different problems confronted in life.

Personal guidance is necessary at all stages of life. At the elementary school stage opportunities should be given to students for their self-expression. Personal guidance at this stage deals with the problems related to feeling of insecurity, social acceptance, discipline etc. At the secondary stage, the students have more intricate personal problems. During the secondary stage adolescent students due to peculiar physical, emotional and social developments undergo noticeable changes in their attitude and behaviour. Personal guidance at this stage should therefore focus on personal and social adjustment. Personal guidance at the tertiary stage aims at helping them view life in relation to reality. The scope of personal guidance at this stage is very wider.

***Educational Guidance*:** If one closely examines the problems of young pupils in schools and colleges, one would exactly realise the need of educational guidance. Educational problems head the needs of students'problems. So, education is an important guidance area. Educational guidance is related to every aspect of education school/ colleges, the curriculum, the methods of instruction, other curricular activities, disciplines etc.

Educational guidance is the assistance given to the individual; (a) to understand his/her potentialities; (b) have a clear cut idea of the different educational opportunities and their requirements; (c) to make-wise choices as regards to school, colleges, the course: curricular and extra-curricular. Some of the aims and objectives of educational guidance are:

(i) To assist the pupil to understand him/herself i.e., to understand his/her potentialities, strength and limitations.
(ii) To help the child make educational plans consist with his/her abilities, interests and goals.

(iii) To enable the student to know detail about the subject and courses offered.
(iv) To assist the student in making satisfactory progress in various school/college subjects.
(v) To help the child to adjust with the schools, its rules, regulations, social life connected with it.
(vi) To help the child in developing good study habits.
(vii) To help the child to participate in out of class educational activities in which he can develop leadership and other social qualities.

At the elementary stage guidance programme must help the children to make good beginning, to plan intelligently, to get the best out of their education and prepare them for secondary schools. Educational guidance needs to be used in diagnosing difficulties, in identifying the special needs of children. At the secondary stage educational guidance should help the pupils to understand themselves better, to understand different aspects of the school, to select appropriate courses to get information about different educational opportunities, to develop good study habits. The students should be helped to be acquainted with the vocational implications of various school subjects. Educational guidance at the tertiary stages must oriented students about purpose and scope of higher studies and helps them to stimulate their studies. Each college/university must have a guidance unit with due provision of guidance services.

Vocational Guidance: You know that bread and butter aims are one of the main aims of education. Due to advancement in science and echnology and consequent charges in industry and occupations have been emerged. There are thousands of specialised jobs/occupations. In this context, there is a great need for vocational guidance. Vocational guidance is a process of assisting the individual to choose an occupation, prepare for it, and enter upon it and progress in it. It is concerned primarily with helping individuals make decisions and choices involved in planning a future and building a career. The purpose behind assisting the youth to choose, prepare, enter and progress in a vocation is the optimum growth of the individual. Some of the aims and objectives of vocational guidance are:

(i) Assisting pupil to discover his/her own abilities and skills to feet them into general requirements of the occupation under consideration.
(ii) Helping the individual to develop an attitude towards work that will dignify whatever type of occupation she may wish to enter.
(iii) Assisting the individual to think critically about various types of occupations and to learn a technique for analysing information about vocations.
(vi) Assisting pupils to secure relevant information about the facilities offered by various educational institutions engaging in vocational training.
(v) At the elementary stage, although no formal guidance programmes are needed, the orientation to vocation can be initiated at this stage. At this stage some qualities and skills which have grater vocational significance viz., (a) love and respect for manual work; (b) training in use of hands; (c) spirit of cooperative work; (d) sharing, (e) appreciation for all works, (f) good interpersonal relationship are to be developed.

At the secondary stage vocational guidance should help the students to know themselves, to know the world of work, to develop employment readiness to develop decision making rules. At the higher education stages it should be more formal one. The objectives of guidance at this stage are to help the students to get information about different career, training facilities, apprenticeship etc.

***Avocational Guidance*:** The individual student spends only a small portion of his time i.e., four to six hours per day in school. The rest of the time needs to be effectively managed and utilised by the child for his/her progress and development. *Avocational guidance* helps the child to judiciously utilise the leisure time. The other co-curricular activities play an important role in all-round development of the child. But many parents; teachers and children put secondary importance to these activities. The students need to be properly guided for effective participation in varied types of avocational pursuits so that they are able to shape their interpersonal behavior in desirable direction and widen their outlook.

Social Guidance: We are social animals. But social relationships constitute a problem area for most of the students. School/educational institution is a miniature society and pupil from different socio-economic status, linguistic and socio-cultural background read there. Students some time may face problems in adjustment and social relationship. It is very important that the students to be helped in acquiring in feeling of security and being accepted by the group; in developing social relationship and in becoming tolerant towards others. This is the task of social guidance. Formally social guidance can be given by educational institutions whereas informal guidance may be provided by family, religious institutions, media etc.

Moral Guidance: Moral values occupy an important place in our life. Some times due to influence of diverse factors students tell lies and indulge in undesirable practices. Moral guidance helps in bringing these students in to proper track and help in their all round development.

Health Guidance: Health is regarded as the wealth. Total health i.e. preventive and curative is the goal of health guidance. The health guidance may be a cooperative effort of Principal, doctors, counsellor/psychologist, teachers, students and parents. For promoting preventive care the conditions of school hostel, canteen needs to be checked. Similarly health education through formal classes and information is essential in school education stages. In the present day the concern of health guidance also pertains to guidance in HIV/AIDs.

Leisure-time guidance: Guidance for leisure is basically a part of personal guidance. The individual should know how to utilise his/her leisure time fruitfully. Leisure generally refers to free time a person at his disposal. Leisure in modern time is available to those who are technically trained and efficient. But, unfortunately most of us do not know how to utilise the leisure time. That is why guidance for leisure is necessary. Leisure can be fruitfully utilized for two purposes. First of all leisure provides us time for personal development. One can increase his efficiency by utilising his leisure time. The second use of leisure is that it helps the individual to be more productive by getting the necessary rest and recreation. Jones divides leisure time activities into four groups.

1. Escape activities,
2. General culture or appreciation activities,
3. Creative activities, and
4. Service activities

It has also been suggested that individuals should spend their leisure time in social welfare activities. For professional growth one must take active interest in the professional society of his profession.

Thus, it is quite evident that guidance for leisure is extremely important in modern society because it helps the individual to attain efficiency and become a useful member of the society. Therefore, it has been suggested that in the school curriculum there should be provision for teaching about various leisure time activities so that children will able to know about them.

3

Types of Guidance

Introduction

In the second chapter, we have gained knowledge of about meaning, importance and areas of guidance. We have also familiar with different school guidance services. One of the services is group guidance service. From the organisation point of view guidance can be of two types, i.e., individual and group. Many institutions/organisations work in the area of guidance and counselling. In this unit, we will learn about importance of group guidance and international, national and state level agencies of guidance.

Objectives

After going through this unit, we should be able to:

(i) Define group guidance,
(ii) Aware of the need and importance of group guidance;
(iii) Know the practical consideration of organisation of group guidance activities;
(iv) Understand the limitations of group guidance activities; and deal effectively with the problems of organisation of such group guidance activities;
(v) State the role and functions of different agencies at international, national and state levels.

(vi) Aware of the need and importance of group guidance;

(vii) Know the practical consideration of organisation of group guidance activities;

(viii) Understand the limitations of group guidance activities; and deal effectively with the problems of organisation of such group guidance activities;

(ix) State the role and functions of different agencies at international, national and state levels.

Types of Guidance

Ther are two types of guidance, namely Individual and Group Guidance. **Individual guidance**

Individual guidance is tailored to an individual. It is advice, strategy or planning designed for a singular person or thing and their unique situation. This is in contrast to general guidance which is frequently-based on demographic information such as age or income or meant for the general population. The most common reference to individual guidance is in reference to children or students. This is ideally the role of guidance, educational counsellors. Individual guidance can be used to refer to any advice, usually professional advice, given to a person based on their unique circumstances. This could include legal services, career counselling, financial planning, medical or psychological advice or a number of other areas where a trained professional is looked to for direction in a given area.

Group Guidance

Concept, Need and Significance : Group refers to collection of people, interaction between individuals, development of shared perceptions, the development of affectiveties and the development of inter-dependence of roles. For example, many students and teacher/teachers at one school may gather together to form a group.

Group guidance encompasses those activities of guidance which are carried on in a group situation to assist its members to have experiences desirable or even necessary for making-appropriate decisions in the prevailing contexts. In a more specific term, it is guiding the individual in a group situation. Group could be of any type, but for guidance purposes a group should have a common goal. Just collection of individual may not be called a group for organising guidance activities. Selection of group members will have to depend on sharing a common problem, volunteering to be members and willingness to group activities. *Jones, A.J.* (1951) define group guidance as any group enterprise or activity in which the primary purpose is to assist each individual in the group to solve his problems and to make his adjustment. Group *guidance* is used to address the developmental needs of a functional group consisting of a number of students to implement programme that would benefit them at all time. Students in group with common problems and concerns are helped in groups i.e., small or large. In other words, if guidance is to be available to all, it should be planned in groups.

Objectives of group guidance are:

1. To help people in identifying common problems, analyse them and find relevant solutions.
2. To place a wide range of information before people with common problems which could be useful for them for finding solutions?
3. To provide a platform where people with common problems could interact with each other and could be benefitted by each other's perspectives, ideas and experiences.
4. To help in creating an atmosphere where people could get an opportunity to express themselves and in the process analyse themselves.

Organistion of Group Guidance Activities

Planning of group guidance activity may focus the following points:

1. ***Need Assessment:*** The need assessment must be done to find out the common problems of individuals in the group. This can be done by administering questionnaire, checklists and interview.
2. ***Determining size of the group and time, venue for group activities:*** Depending upon the group activity the size of the group should be fixed. The size should be approachable and

manageable. The venue should be selected taking in to account the group selected for activity.

3. ***Selection of members and role specifications***: The participants' selection for group guidance activity is also very important. The students for example should be communicated about their roles in group activities.
4. *Orientation of Members:* The group goals should be clarified. It should be stated in clear, objective and measurable terms.
5. ***Monitoring of activities and evaluation of outcomes:*** If we want to conduct the activities purposefully, it should be properly monitored taking into account the goal/s. Feedback about activity needs to be collected from participants.

Some of the common group guidance activities are: Class talk, career talk, displays and exhibitions.

Techniques of Group Guidance

A number of techniques are used in organising group guidance.

Group Discussion: For example, at senior secondary stage, students should have knowledge about different career. A group discussion may be organised in the school. For organisation of the group discussion proper room/hall, group and relevant topic and expert/resource person should be selected. The group discussion will be useful only if the members participate effectively without the fear and all the members have the opportunity to participate. But the effectiveness of the group discussion depends upon the facilitator and the group selected.

Problem solving: For solving individual as well as common problems, problem solving can be applied as a technique. It comprises the following steps:

(i) Existence of common problem,
(ii) Focussed description of the problem,
(iii) Initiation of action for solving problem based on relevant facts,
(iv) Analysis of problem in the light of data collected,
(v) Listing of possible solutions and evaluation of them,
(vi) Acceptance of degree of acceptance of solution in the group.

***Role play*:** In small group, role playing can be adopted as a technique of guidance. Role playing is a method where real life situations are simulated by group members/participants. This provides new insight, intuitions, skills and understanding of opposing viewpoints. The role playing may comprise of the following steps:

(i) Existence of common problem,
(ii) Orientation of group to role playing and the problem,
(iii) Assigning of roles,
(iv) Preparation of other members/audience to observe intelligently,
(v) Assessing the role play,
(vi) Concluding session and feedback,

Other methods like case study and socio-metric technique can be used as group guidance technique.

Advantages of Group Guidance

We have discussed about different activities and approaches of group guidance. Some of the advantages of group guidance are as follows:

- ***Inspires learning and understanding*:** Interaction in group setting inspires learning and understanding of students. The student learns from other member of group.
- ***Saves time and effort:*** Group guidance technique can save time and effort of both the counsellor and students. The time saved can be used for the more difficult and complex problems of students.
- Improvement of student's attitude and behaviour.
- Development of wholesome and helpful awareness of unrecognised needs and problems of students.

Limitations of Group Guidance: Group guidance though serves a useful purpose, but they cannot be taken as a substitute for individual counselling. Group activities serve many of the objectives of the school guidance programme, but not all of these. Further students may feel hesitant to come out with their personal problems in the group. So, in these cases group guidance cannot be of help. Group guidance activities serve useful purposes specially saving in time and effort.

***While organising these activities, some problems that a counsellor may face are mentioned below*:** A rigid type of administration is often a major cause of trouble. Generally, when the counsellor asks for time in the time-table for conducting these guidance activities, he/she may get a discouraging reply, the time table is already full. No periods are free. So, the counsellor is left with no other choice than to take the substitute management period.

Lack of co-operation on part of the administration as well as the staff members may also create problems in organising such activities. Teacher may feel this as an addition burden. Lack of adequate funds is another problem.

Different Levels of Guidance

Different agencies i.e., government and private at international, national and regional level have been doing significant works in the area of guidance. These agencies are working in training/orientation, career guidance services or development of materials for guidance workers/functionaries.

International Level: International Association of Educational and Vocational Guidance (IAEVG) is a world-wide guidance and counselling organisation, whose mission is to promote the development and quality of educational and vocational guidance. IAEVG's mission is also to ensure that all citizens who need and want educational and vocational guidance and counselling can receive this counselling from a competent and recognised professional. The objectives of the organisation are as follows:

(i) To promote communication among persons and organizations active in educational and vocational guidance.

(ii) To encourage the continuing development of ideas, practice and research in the field of guidance and counselling on each level, national and international, in developing and developed countries.

(iii) To advise government and national or international organizations on the development of guidance systems and further the exchange of professionals and experts.

(iv) To collect and disseminate information of interest in the field of educational and vocational guidance practice, study and research

The Mission of IAEVG is to

(a) Advocate that all citizens who need and want educational and vocational guidance and counselling can receive this counselling from a competent and recognised professional.
(b) Recommend the basic nature and quality of service that should typify the service provided to students and adults.
(c) Recommend the essential training and other qualifications that all counsellors in educational and vocational guidance should have.
(d) Urge governments to enhance, facilitate or establish an agency, institution, or office with responsibility to develop and maintain.
(e) Policies governing the provision of educational and vocaitonal guidance.
(f) The provision of training and continuing education programs for counselling and guidance practitioners.
(g) The development and provision of appropriate and effective methods and materials for guidance.
(h) The conduct of research and development to create new, more comprehensive, and better ways of conducting educational and vocational guidance.
(i) The development of appropriate methods of evaluation af counselling and guidance.

The Association publishes a newsletter three times a year. Furthermore, IAEVG publishes the International Journal for Educational and Vocational Guidance which is a referred journal publishing articles in relation to work and leisure, career development, career counselling and guidance and career education.

The website can be found at www.iaevg.org/

Cedefop, the European Agency to promote the development of vocational education and training, is the European Union's centre of expertise to support the development of VET and evidence-based policy-making. One important task for Cedefop is to provide guidance practitioners with advice, research, analysis and information. On Cedefop's website European Training Village (ETV), there is an area with information on lifelong guidance (Choose life-long guidance in the left menu). Here you will find information on European guidance projects, links to publications and research results, examples of good guidance strategies and practices and a live network for all the actors who have an interest in the field.

Fedora is an organisation for those involved in student guidance in institutions of higher education in Europe. The Fedora network has especially the focus on the higher student mobility across Europe and the challenges that give to the guidance practitioners. Fedora contributes to the further development of the guidance practitioners competencies so they can better support, inform and guide the students on mobility issues. Fedora organises congresses, conferences and summer universities and each event takes place every three years. All types of events take place in different countries in the Fedora member states each year.

IAC (*International Association for Counselling*): wishes to encourage the exchange of ideas, research findings and personal experience in the field of counselling and guidance. This happens, among others, through organising conferences and publishing the International Journal for the Advancement of Counselling.

The International Centre for Career Development and Public Policy *(ICCDPP)* has the task to facilitate international sharing of knowledge and information concerning public policy and career development issues. ICCDPP has a base for knowledge and information which contains proceedings from international symposia, and reports and news provided to the site by the users and by other international contacts. ICCDPP is supported by OECD, the World Bank, and the European Commission etc.

The Nordic Association of Educational and Vocational Guidance are a coalition of national associations for education and vocational guidance in the Nordic countries and the self-governing areas of Aaland Islands and Faeroe Islands. The aim of NFUE is to strengthen professional educational and vocational guidance in Nordic countries.

NAEVG organises seminars and conferences and develops co-operation with the Baltic countries. The website can be found at www.nfsy.org

The European Lifelong Guidance Policy Network aims to assist the European Union Member States and the Commission in moving European co-operation on lifelong guidance forward in both the education and the employment sectors. The purpose is to promote co-operation at Member State level on lifelong guidance and to propose appropriate structures and support mechanisms in implementing the priorities identified in the Resolution on Lifelong Guidance (2004). The ELGPN was established by the Member States and the Commission has foreseen to support the activities of the network in 2007-2008 under the Lifelong Learning Programme.

***International Labour Organisation* (ILO):** The ILO is the international organisation responsible for drawing up and overseeing international labour standards. It is the only 'tripartite' United Nations agency that brings together representatives of governments, employers and workers to jointly shape policies and programmes promoting, 'Decent Work for all'. This unique arrangement gives the ILO an edge in incorporating 'real world' knowledge about employment and work.The organisation publishes the results of research related to changing nature of work and employment which is important for policy makers and other users.

National Level Agencies: At national level the following organisations work in the area of guidance and counselling.

***National Council of Educational Research and Training (NCERT)*:** The Department of Psychology and Foundation of Education (DEPFE), a Department under NCERT, New Delhi and Pandit Sunderlal Sharma Central Institute of Vocational Education (PSSCIVE), Bhopal a constituent of NCERT organise programme on guidance and counselling. Some of the functions of PSSCIVE are:

To advise and assist the Ministry of Human Resource Development, State Governments and Union Territory Administration in the implementation of the Vocational Education and Work Experience Programme.

(i) To function as the technical wing of the Joint Council of Vocational Education on all matters relating to Vocational Education Programme (VEP).
(ii) To promote, supervise and guide the establishment of a comprehensive management system for VEP.
(iii) To serve as a resource institution for both formal and non-formal VEP.
(iv) To orient and train various key functionaries of VEP, including teachers.
(v) To evaluate and monitor VEP in States/UTs.
(vi) To ensure uniformity and maintain quality standards in vocational teaching and learning.
(vii) To provide guidance and counselling on Vocational Education and Training to the people at large.

DEPFE is the department of NCERT which coordinates guidance activities in the country. The department runs an International Diploma Course in Guidance and Counselling in collaboration with Commonwealth of Learning, Canada. This course is offered at the Department of Educational Psychology and Foundations of Education (DEPFE), NCERT New Delhi as well as five Regional Institutes of Education located at Bhubaneswar Bhopal, Mysore, Shillong, and Ajmer. Besides, the department conducts training programme in the field of guidance and counselling.

Central Institute for Research and Training in Employment Service *(CIRTES)* was establihsed in October, 1964 under the *aegis* of the director and General of Employment and Training (DGE&T) and Ministry of Labour, government of India. In 1971 and 1987, the institute was expanded with added responsibilities of developing in career literature and to provide guidance for the promotion of self-employment.

The main objectives of CIRTES are:

(i) Planning and conducting training programmes for Employment Service Personnel at State, National and International Levels.
(ii) Conducting research into problems concerning the activities of the Employment Service.
(iii) Development and publication of career literature and audio-visual aids for use in Vocational Guidance and Career Literature Programmes.
(iv) Development of motivational material for promotion of self-employment.

There are four divisions of CIRTES i.e., training division, research division, and career study center and self-employment guidance cell.

1. ***Training Division:*** Training Division caters to the training needs of all the Employment Officers of the country in placement, vocational guidance, employment market information, self-employment promotional activities and other related matters. Instructional materials and training aids are devised and developed to assist the States in organising training programmes for the staff of their employment exchanges. Besides, special training programmes for the employment officers of foreign countries under various ILO bilateral programmes are organised on request basis. The Division also associates with other training organisations for imparting training in the field of vocational guidance and self-employment.
2. ***Research Division:*** Research Division conducts studies on organisational, operational and procedural aspects of NES, labour-market conditions and other related matters. Development of various tools and techniques and evaluation of various programmes of NES *inter alia* come under its purview.
3. ***Career Study Centre (CSC):*** CSC develops and publishes the career literature in the shape of bookelets and pamphlets/folders on various careers/occupations covering their job content, educational preparatory requirements, employment and self-employment opportunities, as a reference tool to meet the career

planning needs of students, job seekers, Vocational Guidance Officers/Counsellors and others. These publications are disseminated to Employment Exchanges, University Employment Information and Guidance Bureaux (UEIGBx), Coaching-cum-Guidance Centre for SC/ST, colleges, schools and also to other agencies engaged in vocational guidance activities, through Employment Exchanges as per their jurisdiction.

4. ***Self-employment Guidance Cell (SEGC):*** SEGC prepares informative and motivational material to assist Employment Officers in guiding and confidence building among job seekers for adopting self-employment ventures. It also provides training to the Employment Officers on self-employment promotional related activities. directorate General of employment and Training (DGE&T), under Ministry of Labour evolves policy and standards for vocational guidance activities through employment exchanges. Other organizations like *University Grants Commission* (UGC), *All India Council of Technical Education* (AICTE) also works on guidance and counselling.

State Level Agencies of Guidance: At state level *SCERT*, Bureau of Educational and Vocational Guidance, Directorates of Employment work for guidance of students. SCERT/State Guidance Bureaus coordinates guidance services at the state level. They organise state level training./orientation for guidance personnel. State Directorates of Employment co-ordinates vocational guidance programme through employment exchanges in states.They also develop publication on occupational information.

Universities: In university employment bureaus facilities are provided for students. At the local level some district employment exchanges, private agencies and institutional level organisations work for guidance and counselling. The role of NGOs at different level for providing guidance activities is also very important.

4

Career Guidance Work and Mental Health

Introduction

Work has evolved a lot since the industrial revolution partly due to the progress of sciences and technologies. Major transformations happened in the organisational structure and culture, with their consequences on the organisations of work.

Meaning of Work

Work is life, idleness is death. With a few exceptions, nearly everyone has to work in order to make a living. The most obvious reason to work is the sheer necessity for survival. For those who wish to live a more **affluent life,** they work harder and longer to get extra income or overtime **remuneration. Work,** then, is equivalent to a higher standard of living.

Work is either paid or unpaid. Paid work is what most people associate with team-work.

Unpaid work, includes housework and school work. Most people in full time employment work five days a week, although there has been an increase in the number of people working at weekends and part time. In recent years, the ability to work flexible hours has grown it's importance.

People do not necessarily enjoy work but they all enjoy the reward of their work and the reward is so tangible and immediate that no one can fail to appreciate it. Therefore, it can be said that the primary objective of the multitude to work is for survival and for tangible material reward.

***Major approaches to study of meaning of work*:** There are three major approaches to the study of the meaning of work, the definitions of work, the orientations of work and the coherence of work. As such we can define the meaning of work in three ways.

The Significance of Work

The concept of meaning of work can be defined as the significance of the subject attributes to work, his representation of work, and the importance it has in his life. Work is central in many cultures, although every culture has its own values and conceptions about it. However, it seems that work is important and significant for a majority of people considering the time that individuals devote to work in their lives, the numerous functions which it accomplishes for them and the fact that work is closely linked with other important aspects of daily life such as family, leisure, religion and community life.

The notion of work has several definitions but they all share the idea of a purposeful activity. This notion generally refers to expanding energy through a set of co-ordinated activities aimed at producing something useful. Work may be pleasant or unpleasant and may or may not be associated with monetary exchanges. Moreover it does not necessarily have to be accomplished in the context of a job.

Meaning of compensation: In financial terms, the salary and wages you pay to your employees for the work they do, no financial forms of compensation can also be offered to attract and retain staff. Ask any human resources consultant where financial compensation ranks in the hierarchy of employee requirements, and you're likely to get a range of answers. Some say it's the most important thing others declare wages are the only important thing. Still others say that while financial compensation isn't the most important thing it's important enough that if your paid isn't fair, all the other employee benefits in the world may not be enough to keep employees on board.

Obviously, it's important to know whether you are paying enough and how to get the most for what you are paying. In addition, you have to know how to *bolster* the actual dollars you lay out in salary and wages with non financial compensation. You don't pay employees in a vaccum. That's another way of saying that the level of compensation that will attract and keep employees is set primarily by other employers. While there's no formula that will tell you the ideal salary for each position within your company there are appropriate ranges.

Some of the key sources for determining suitable salary ranges for your employees are:

1. Classified advertisement listings for specific positions both in your daily newspaper and on the internet.
2. Professional and trade organisations for the specific fields in which you're hiring. Most organisations regularly publish salary data.
3. Human resources consultants.
4. Specialised recruiters in the appropriate fields.

While no one can discount the importance of financial rewards, keep in mind that today's job candidates are more concerned with corporate environment and quality of life issues than over before. In our executive survey, conducted by *Robert Half, International Corporate Culture rivaled* employee benefits are important for candidates during job interviews. Many small businesses use this trend as a competitive advantage, offering such non financial perks as flexible work schedules, casual dress days, additional vacation time and tele commuting opportunities. The costs of this approach are minimal, particularly when compared to the value added benefits of improved recruitment, productivity and retention. Regardless of the monetary and non-monetary ways you compensate your employees, creating an employee-friendly environment and determining competitive compensation ranges take time. Both require being flexible and adaptable to changing workplace trends and local conditions. The investment is worth the difference between a good company and a great company is its people.

Meaning of Incentive

A reward for a specific behavior designed to encourage that behavior also called inducements. Can you motivate employees during a recession with a successful employee incentive plan? By *Stuart Jennings: Bonus* plans Pay for performance programs MBO programme commission plans stock option stock appreciation rights. Employee incentive plans go by many different names, you've undoubtedly seen your share. But, with our economy struggling, how should you approach your employee incentive plans differently to reach your organisations goals? Or can an employee incentive plan actually create the results you need?

Relation between Work and Leisure, Work and Incentives

Work and Leisure Work: Work plays a major role in people's like. When you think of work there are several definitions depending upon your own experiences and the society in which you live. In western societies, paid employment is considered to be the most important type of work. Work is socially defined and needs to be understood in particular contexts work provides an individual with income, self identity and status.

Leisure: Leisure is also an important aspect of people's lives. Leisure activities are those associated with the beach, outdoor living and sport and form an important part of an Australian identity. Leisure can be defined as time not spent working or meeting the necessaries of life. It is also linked to quality of life issues. There is strong relationship between the type of work an individual does and the way they spend their leisure time. Leisure has become a commodity to be purchased and these results in the exclusion of some groups in society. Market forces exclude the unemployed, the poor and elderly from participation.

Leisure can be divided in active and passive forms:

Inter-relationship between work and leisure: The differentiation between work and leisure is basic to all definitions. Generally, work is understood to be remunerative, required by social norms and necessary for the maintenance of the self and family.

Leisure is non-work i.e., leisure is not remunerative, not required by social expectations, and not necessary for status or survival. However, all non-work is not considered leisure. The relationship between work and leisure-work is dependent upon quality of life issues and varies with each individual depending upon their choice of work. For some groups of people leisure is an extension of their work activities. Leisure activities are related to job satisfaction and involvement in work. Work also provides the financial means with which to participate in leisure. Leisure activities engaged in by individuals are dependent on the work undertaken and level of education. Professional sports people engage in leisure activate and also receive monetary payments. For some people the skills they have also extend into a means of earning a living. Educational institutions provide individuals with necessary skills and the means to participate in meaningful employment. This in turn also influences the types of leisure activities undertaken and often provides status, control and a degree of choice about participation in leisure activities. The media is increasingly influencing leisure activities.

Relationship between Work and Incentives

Managing employee performance is steadily rising to the top of many senior leaders agendas. The fast pace of business, an ultra-competitive marketplace and increasing customer demands have made it difficult for leaders to quickly and effectively respond to ever-changing market conditions. Compounded by declining workforce productivity, escalating employee disengagement and the forthcoming retirement of seventy six million baby boomers, companies are being forced to finally focus their attention on their most valuable assets: their employees. Corporations worldwide are scrambling to find effective ways to attract and retain the best talent, but also to elevate their performance, productivity and service levels to new heights. Embodied in this quest is the ability to align individual behaviors with strategic corporate objectives and, importantly, to motivate and reward those who meet or exceed those objectives. In today's business climate, organisations must achieve maximum Return on Investment (ROI) in their people to boost corporate performance and gain a competitive advantage. The new 'must have' Employee performance is everything – it's what distinguishes top performing companies from those who are struggling. Statistics show that companies who recognise their people outperform companies that don't by thirty to forty per cent. Businesses are beginning to understand the value of investing resources to establish, market and support improved performance improvement strategies for one compelling reason: satisfied, motivated and dedicated individuals are increasingly critical to corporate survival and imperative for growth.

Recognition and incentive programs are rarely mentioned in the context of that conversation, despite the fact that seventy eight per cent of companies have at least one performance-related program in place. This must change if leaders expect to take advantage of the full arsenal of tools available to help them achieve their corporate objectives. Research is proving that recognition and incentive programs are powerful and effective vehicles for boosting corporate performance and the bottom line.

Smart Human Resource executives are taking the cue and expanding their portfolio of solutions to include incentive programs, as well as recognition programs in that **arsenal**. Incentives are commonly associated with sales initiatives; so few professionals outside of the sales arena have fully embraced them as tried-and-true methods for raising overall employee productivity. This is a missed opportunity because we have learned that incentive programs can be used to inspire employees throughout the enterprise. A recent study found that eighty eight to ninety five per cent of all incentive programs reach or exceed their goals, and that the ROI on non-sales employee programs (200 per cent) is actually greater than the ROI on incentives directed to sales staff (134 per cent).

Exploring the broader use of incentives compliments another innovative corporate trend – aligning internal and external branding efforts to maximise customer satisfaction and profitability. Internal branding is defined as motivating internal audiences (employees) to deliver the quality service promised by advertising and sales. Research by The Forum for People Performance Management and Measurement at Northwestern University discovered a direct link between employee satisfaction, customer satisfaction, and a company's profitability, even when the employees did not have direct customer contact. If you want employees to understand the corporate message and to treat your customers the right way, you have to set the example by making sure they have that message and they're treated with the same care and respect you want them to demonstrate to customers. Internal branding also thrusts motivation and performance improvement into the C—suite because brand equity is a C—level priority, giving HR professionals an opportunity to demonstrate the strategic value of recognition to the CEO.

Proven results: C-suite interest we now have a growing body of compelling research from credible sources around the world on the positive – and significant – impact of recognition and incentive programs on a company's financial performance. The research demonstrates that companies who engage in incentive and recognition programs are significantly outperforming their competitors (who don't run programs) in bottom line savings, contributions to the profit line and shareholder return. This is important news for companies seeking every possible advantage in the market-place. The research has attracted the attention of business leaders and helped them to realise that everyone in their company is affecting the organisation's ability to compete and thrive. There's no better vehicle for a CEO to communicate what's important to the company than to recognise and reward people for the behaviors and results that drive the company towards success. Recognition programs have proven to be a highly effective means of aligning the boardroom and the lunchroom and *cascading* the company's strategic imperatives throughout the organisation and into the hands of the people who can make them a reality.... people who are often anxious to make a meaningful contribution. Maximising ROI Frequently, companies run a number of disparate recognition and incentive programs that span various departments. A common approach has been to allow each department to implement a unique program with goals and rewards specific to the individuals in that unit.

However, when you have independent programs within an organisation there is often poor accountability for ROI or clear line of sight to overall results. Most companies don't really know how much they're actually spending on programs let alone how much value they're extracting from them. Running a multitude of disparate programs also undermines the opportunity for creating a consistent, over-arching performance-based culture throughout the company. Additionally, there's the danger that employees will perceive that one department is favored over another or that some managers are offering more generous awards.

Companies are consolidating many of their programs to decrease expenses and increase effectiveness. Multiple programs are being pulled into one corporate-wide program with numerous sub-programs and variations to address the specific needs of different business units or geographical locations. This consolidation helps strip-out cost and administrative burden while insuring a unified message and application throughout the enterprise. Organisations are also becoming much more aware of all the contributors to corporate success and are implementing performance and recognition programs to help align and recognise more employees for their contributions to those successes. Employers have realised that everyone in the company – not just the sales team – can contribute to revenue growth and operational efficiencies that help a company prosper. Leaders need to gain the support and buy-in from everyone who can influence company results. Keep in mind that if you're not actively engaging employees in your goals, they may be working against your efforts – even if it's done unintentionally and inadvertently. Now a days, some of those additional participants are likely to be based around the world. The internet allows us to easily execute programs across borders and many HR professionals are delighted to finally be able to offer something better than watered down versions of their domestic programs to those employees who live and work beyond the corporate office. Offshore employees are pushing for these programs as well, unwilling to be bystanders in the company's recognition efforts any longer. Online program technology does the heavy lifting of language translation, currency conversions, and creating multiple award catalogs that reflect the brands and types of awards that will be compelling and relevant in different countries. Track and measure

Demand is rising steadily for more measurement in recognition and incentive programs. Companies are looking to reward the quantifiable, actionable behaviors of their employees and more metrics are being introduced into programs. There's also a growing interest in tracking program performance throughout its course, rather than waiting until the end to assess the results. Sales incentive programs have always been focused on measurement, usually on revenue growth or sales.

Traditionally, recognition programs have been more discretionary: you catch someone doing something beyond the call of duty and reward them. Now many recognition programs are also focusing on very specific corporate goals or initiatives to avoid being viewed as an entitlement or risking programs being eliminated due to ambiguous results.

Tracking metrics during the program allows you to quantify the end result and also affect the outcome, you can intercede if a group is not performing well and provide extra-training or assistance. Or, you can spread the word about a successful initiative so that everyone can benefit from the example.

Inspire, reward and achieve: As workplaces change, employees are asked to adapt, learn, re-adapt, and re-learn in order to ensure that companies themselves retain a competitive edge. Recognising these employees for service, achievement or performance is vital to corporate health. A well-known veteran of recognition, *Herb Kelleher, former CEO of Southwest* Airlines believes that anyone, who looks at things solely in terms of factors that can easily be quantified, is missing the heart of the business, which is people. Herb has it exactly right on a number of levels. First, as companies have automated their back offices with Enterprise Resource Planning (ERP) solutions and implemented Customer Relationship and Supply Chain Management systems (CRM), they have benefited significantly from the efficiencies and cost savings of these applications.

The next big thing is to focus on implementing and improving those processes and programs that manage our people assets. Recognition and incentive programs are a proven, strategic opportunity to do just that. Few initiatives can deliver such significant ROI and also advance the company's reputation as a great place to work in the process.

Secondly, as people performance is increasingly being recognised as the means with which companies can gain competitive edge, people are also identified as the method to achieving those results. As more and more leaders make the shift to a strategic view of recognition and incentives, and the powerful dynamics of rewarding those individuals who directly contribute to the success of the organisation, the gap will widen between the companies who thrive and those that will struggle or disappear.

Outdated view and Strategic view

(i) Employees as expenses,
(ii) Employees as assets and profit drivers;
(iii) Recognition and incentive programs as a discretionary cost; Recognition and incentive programs as a major source of shareholder value;
(iv) Recognition and incentive program owners as administrators.

Recognition and incentive program owners as thought leaders; and finally, Herb's words remind us that the people we influence with recognition and incentive programs are busy spending their day influencing other vital corporate assets – customers! The link between customer satisfaction and loyalty, and employee satisfaction and loyalty has been firmly established: happy customers are a result of happy and engaged employees. That means that putting performance programs to work for you is far more than a nice idea. It's the strategic and profitable thing to do.

Meaning, Characteristics and Need for Mental Health

It has always been easier to define mental illnesses than to define mental health. More recently many have recognised that mental health is more than the absence of mental illness. Even though many of us don't suffer from a diagnosable mental disorder, it is clean that some of us are mentally disorder it is clear that some of us are mentally healthier than others.

Definition and Meaning of Mental Health

Mental health is a concept that refers to a human individual's emotional, psychological and intellectual well being. A branch of medicine that deal with the achievements and maintenance of psychological well-being.

Definition: A state of emotional and psychological well-being in which an individual is able to use his or her cognitive and emotional capabilities function in society, and meet the ordinary demands of everyday life.

Dianne Hales and Robert Hales define mental Health as the capacity to think rationally and logically and to cope with the transitions, stresses, traumas and losses that occur in all lives, in ways that allow emotional stability and growth. In general mentally healthy individuals value themselves, perceive reality as it is, accept its limitation and possibilities, respond to its challenges carry out their responsibilities, establish and maintain close relationships, deal reasonably with others, pursue work that suits their talent and training and feel sense of fulfillment that makes the efforts of daily living worthwhile.

Definitions of mental health are changing. It used to be that a person was considered to have good mental health simply if they showed no signs or symptoms of a mental illness. But in recent years there has been a shift towards a more holistic approach to mental health. Today we recognise that good mental health is not just the absence of mental illness. Nor is it absolute – some people are more mentally healthy than others, whether you are mentally ill or not. These realisations are promoting a new kind of focus on mental health that identifies components of mental wellness and mental fitness and explore ways to encourage them.

It is commonly known in the mental health field that in order to achieve good mental health, you also need a healthy dose of self esteem. However, what has not been stressed adequately is the importance and need to nurture such traits such as positive emotional wellness, optimism, memories and happiness.

Characteristics of Mental Health

***Ability to enjoy life*:** The ability to enjoy life is essential to good mental health; can you live in the moment and appreciate the now.

Are you able to learn from the past and plan for the future without dwelling on things you can't change or predict James Taylor wrote that the secret of life is enjoying the passing of time? Any fool can do it. There ain't nothing to it. The practice of mindfulness, meditation is one way to cultivate the ability to enjoy the present. We of course need to plan for the future at times and we also need to learn from the past. Too often we make ourselves miserable in the present by worrying about the future.

Resilience: The ability to bounce back from adversity has been referred to as resilience. Are you able to bounce back from hard times? Can you manage the stress of a serious life event without losing your optimism and a sense of perspective? It has been long known that some people handle stress better than others, why do some adults raised in alcoholic families do well, while others have repeated problems in life? The characteristic of resilience is shared by those who cope well with stress.

***Balance*:** Balance in life seems to result in greater mental health. Are you able to juggle the many aspects of your life? Can you recognise when you might be devoting too much time to one aspect, at the expense of others? Are you able to make changes to restore balance when necessary? We all need to balance time spent socially with time spent alone, e.g., those who spend all of their time alone may get labelled as loners and they may lose many of their social skills. Extreme social isolation may even result in a split with reality. Those who ignore the need for some solitary times also risk such a split. Balance these two needs seems to be the key although we all balance these differently. Other areas where balance seems to be important include the balance between work and play, the balance between sleep and wakefulness, the balance between rest and exercise, and even the balance between time spent indoors and time spent outdoors.

Flexibility: Do you feel and express a range of emotions? When problems arise can you change your expectations – of life, others, and yourself to solve the problem and feel better? We all know some people hold very rigid opinions. No amount of discussion can change their views.

Such people often set themselves up for added stress by the rigid expectations that they hold working on making our expectations more flexible can improve our mental health.

Mentally healthy people experience a range of emotions and allow themselves to express their feelings. Some people shut off certain feelings finding them to be unacceptable. This emotional rigidity may result in other mental health problems.

Self-actualisation: Do you recognise and develop your strengths so that you can reach your full potential? What have we made of the gifts that we have been given? We all know people who have surpassed their potential and others who seem to have *squandered* their gifts. We first need to recognise our gifts, of course, and the process of recognition is part of the path toward self actualisation. Mentally healthy persons are in the process of actualising their potential. In order to do this we must first feel secure. There are just a few of the concepts that are important in attempting to define mental health. The ability to form healthy relationships with others is also important. Adult and Adolescent mental health also includes the concepts of self esteem and healthy sexuality. How we deal with loss and death to also an important of mental health. Mental Health is more than just the absence of mental illness. It includes how you feel about yourself and how you adjust to life events. However, the National Mental Health Association cites ten characteristics of people who are mentally healthy.

(i) They feel good about themselves.
(ii) They do not become overwhelmed by emotions such as fear, anger, love, jealousy, guilt or anxiety.
(iii) They have lasting and satisfying personal relationships.
(iv) They feel comfortable with other people.
(v) They can laugh at themselves and with others.
(vi) They have respect for themselves and for others even if there are differences.
(vii) They are able to accept life's disappointments.
(viii) They can meet life's demands and handle their problems when they arise.
(ix) They make their own decisions.
(x) They shape their environment whenever possible and adjust to it when necessary.

Need for Mental Health: Many people are reluctant to use mental health services because of the stigma of having an emotional problem. Society has a tendency to view mental health issues differently from medical ones. When someone breaks a leg, has chest plains, or needs to get a prescription, they'll see a doctor. However, when they experience depression, excessive fears, or a problem with alcohol, they may be embarrassed to seek help. Many people view these conditions as weaknessess they should handle themselves, unfortunately, this view prevents them for getting professional assistance that may alleviate their problems. To recognise an emotional problem and receive help is not at all a sign of weakness. Rather, these positive actions are characteristics of strong individuals. Also, seeing a therapist at a mental health clinic or student counselling centre is completely confidential. No information will be released without your permission except in situations involving child, or elder abuser or suicidal intent.

Role of Guidance Personnel in Promoting and Preserving Mental Health

The main purpose of the Mental Health Act is to provide authority, criteria and procedures for involuntary admission and treatment. However, the Act also contains protections to ensure that these provisions are applied in an appropriate and lawful manner. Safeguards for the rights of people involuntarily admitted to a psychiatric facility include rights notification, medical examinations at specified time periods, second medical opinions on proposed treatment and access to review panels and the court guide to the Mental Health Act 2.

Most people in British Columbia requiring hospital treatment for mental disorders are voluntarily admitted to hospital, just like people with other illnesses. A sizeable number of people with serious mental disorders, however, refuse to accept psychiatric treatment. (In 2003 there were approximately 8,000 involuntary admissions). Without involuntary admission and treatment made possible by the Mental Health Act, these seriously mentally ill people would continue to suffer, causing significant disruption and harm to their lives and the lives of others.

With involuntary hospital admission and treatment, most people quickly improve to the point that they can continue as voluntary patients or resume their lives in the community. The majority of people involuntarily admitted are discharged within one month. A person can only be admitted as an involuntary patient under the Mental Health Act to facilities designated by the Minister of Health. The term designated facility in the Act and in this Guide refers to designated inpatient; provincial mental health facilities, psychiatric units and observation units.

Observation units are short stay units in small hospitals, where the person is stabilised within a few days and, if continuing inpatient treatment is necessary, transferred. Section 22(7) of the Act and Section 2(2) of the Regulation require that a patient admitted to an observation unit must be transferred to a Provincial mental health facility or a psychiatric unit within five days after a second Medical Certificate is received by the director of the observation unit. This transfer requirement applies only to patients who need further inpatient care and does not apply if the patient is discharged, or released on extended leave (Section 6.0).

There is no legal authority for a hospital or any other health care facility that has not been designated as a provincial mental health facility or a psychiatric unit or observation unit to hold or admit a person for whom a Medical Certificate has been completed. The hospital or certifying physician may have the patient transported to the designated facility. It is the mutual obligation of the closest designated facility and the non-designated hospital to find a bed for the patient.

A non-designated hospital should only care for the patient while in transit to a designated facility. As an example, it is usually preferable to temporarily admit to hospital someone awaiting transportation to a psychiatric unit than to hold them in a jail cell. Non-designated hospitals are advised to develop protocols with the closest designated facility. The person responsible for the operation of a designated facility is referred to in the Mental Health Act as the director.The director is responsible for ensuring each patient is provided with professional service, care and treatment appropriate to the patient's condition (Section 8 of the Act). Three Guide to the Mental Health Act Job stress can be defined as the harmful physical and emotional response that occurs when the requirements of the job do not match the capabilities, resources or needs of the worker. Job stress can cause poor health and can increase rates of work-related injuries and accidents.

Some potential causes of work related stress are overwork, lack of clear instructions, unrealistic deadlines, lack of decision-making, job insecurity, isolated working conditions, surveillance, and inadequate child-care arrangements Although sexual harassment and discrimination are often excluded from lists of traditional job stressors, they must be included in any comprehensive analysis of the causes of workplace stress.

Sexual harassment is a stressor for women in the workplace; and discrimination is a stronger predictor of health outcomes, including mental ill-health, for ethnic minorities than traditional job stressors. Some of the many effects of stress include numerous physical ailments as well as mental health problems such as depression and increased rates of other possible stress-reducing accommodations include:

(i) Altering the pace of work;
(ii) Lowering the noise level of work;
(iii) Providing water, tea or soda and crushed ice to combat a dry mouth caused by some medications;
(iv) Extra-encouragement and praise of job performance, but only if warranted and not obviously excessive;
(v) While taking steps to reduce stress, avoidance of over-protection of the employee;
(vi) Making sure the employee is treated as a member of the team and not excluded from social events, business meetings or other activities relevant to the job. Mental health at work should you mention your panic attacks at the interview? Can you take time off sick with depression? What are the pros and cons of telling your employer, and what are your rights?

If you have a mental health condition such as depression, anxiety or bi-polar disorder, you may not feel you want to tell current or prospective employers. When mental health charity Rethink surveyed 3,000 mental health service users, half the respondents said they felt they had to hide their health problems and forty one per cent were put off applying for jobs in the first place. But it doesn't have to be like that. Good employers realise that a staff member who has experienced mental illness such as depression can be an asset. They often have a better understanding of their own strengths and weaknesses and can help and support other members of staff with similar problems. And new legislation currently going through the House of Lords means you won't have to answer questions about your health before being offered a job.

Positive employers

Some employers go out of their way to show their commitment to equal opportunities. For example, over 590 organisations have signed up to the Mindful Employer Charter for Employers, who are Positive about Mental Health. Jobcentre Plus awards the 'two ticks' symbol to companies in England, Scotland and Wales who have shown they are positive about employing disabled people, which applies to some mental health conditions, and committed to supporting their needs in the workplace. "Having experience of mental distress does not mean you can't have a successful career"

"This doesn't mean employers who aren't involved in the scheme can't be supportive," says Emma Mamo, senior policy and campaigns officer at mental health charity Mind. "The important thing to remember is that having experience of mental distress does not mean you can't have a successful career. Many high achievers have a mental health problem so if you're a career-driven person, don't let it stop you from pursuing your chosen path."

Support in the Work Place

"One in four people experience a mental health problem in any one year, so it's by no means rare to develop a problem while you are at work," says Emma. "Telling your employer what you are going through can help them to support you through tough times. Employers will often work with individuals to make adjustments that are mutually beneficial, for example support managing your workload, working from home, or even small things like changing where your desk is."

"If you qualify for protection under the Disability Discrimination Act, your employer should make reasonable adjustments to support you in the workplace. This could include relaxing absence rules and limits, or allowing you to work flexi hours to make up the time."

The Legal Situation

(i) An amendment to the *Equality Bill* bans employers from asking applicants about their health until after a job offer has been made. Under this legislation, you can choose to tell a prospective employer that you have a mental health condition, for example if they are part of the 'two ticks' scheme, but they can't ask about it at the application or interview stage.

(ii) Information about your mental health is considered to be 'sensitive personal data' under data protection legislation. Employers should ensure only appropriate access is given to any information they hold about your mental health.

(iii) The main body of legislation concerning unfair treatment in the workplace is the *Disability Discrimination Act 1995,* which covers mental illness and related problems. Your employer has a duty to ensure the health, safety, and welfare of their employees, and must not discriminate against mentally ill/ disabled staff or applicants (provided they employ more than fifteen people). If you're worried about your rights or feel you're experiencing discrimination, you can get advice from your local *Citizens Advice Bureau,* your trade union if you belong to one.

(iv) If you think you have been unfairly dismissed, you can take your employer to a tribunal, but you must act quickly as there's a three-month time limit.

Directors are appointed by the authority, usually a health authority (i.e., the Board), operating the designated facility (Section 3 of the Regulation). The director may authorise specific individuals or positions to carry out the director functions. For example, physicians may be authorised to admit and discharge. The senior nurse on duty in the hospital or the ward or a physician could be authorised to sign consent forms for involuntary treatment or warrants after regular business hours. These authorizations should be in written form, signed by the director.

5

Vocational Guidance

Introduction

We all will agree that in recent time there are varieties of educational streams as new occupational opportunities are coming every other day. As there is variety of occupational opportunities available to the students, it is not always possible for students to meet the requirements of the available opportunities as all individual differ in the abilities, interest, attitude and skill from each other. Thus, it is very necessary to know about ones own abilities, skills etc. To help in this process the role of vocational guidance becomes very important. In this unit we will discuss about vocational guidance, and other phenomenon related to the vocational guidance.

Nature and Scope of Vocational Guidance

Concept of vocational guidance: Vocational guidance according to *DAW is that* which have to be made well before the school leaving stage. Indeed with comprehensive education potentially offering a greater educational opportunity a good case for an increasingly important role for vocational guidance can be made. It is worthwhile to look at some of the concepts or frames of refences that are fundamental to a consideration of occupational choice. *Crites* suggest that there are five sets of concepts that need to be considered. Firstly, how far is occupational choice the result of systematic behavior as opposed to chance? Clearly the practice of vocational guidance is concerned with systematising choice. Thus, vocational guidance is not only adjustment but also achievement and development of the individuals to the maximum extent to be successful in their chosen occupations to be satisfied and usefull to the society. Let us discuss the objectives of vocational guidance:

(i) To assist the student to know about the characteristics, functions, duties of the occupations of his choice.
(ii) To enable him to find out what are the specific criteria as skills, abilities, age etc., are required for the occupations of his choice.
(iii) To assist the student to know about his skills, abilities, interests for making-wise choices.
(iv) To assist the student to acquire the technique of analysis before making any final choice.
(v) To provide opportunity for experiences in school and out of school this may provide an idea of the work environment to the student.
(vi) To help the student realise that all honest labour is worthwhile.

The recommendations of *Education Commission set-up* by Government of India in 1964 indicated the aims and scope of vocational guidance. These recommendations suggest the following:

The aim of guidance is not just to help student in making vocational choices but also be focussed on the development of the child as good citizen.

Guidance should be provided in solving learning difficulties, academic excellence, developing study habits and must be started at the primary stage itself.

Guidance role is very crucial at the college level as at this stage student faces many problems related to educational, vocational and personal. They should be making aware about the job market and how to make adjustment in it.

Information may provide about the training, competitive examinations and scholarships available.

Need and Function of Vocational Guidance

Bringing individuals at par with the demands of the jobs:

As we all know that individual differences exist among all and no two individuals can have the same abilities, skills and personalities. We can understand it with an example as a person can be skilled in doing a desk job while the other can be skilled in the field job so the skill differs and thus the demand for the job also different from different individuals. Thus, here vocational guidance is needed for matching the right job with right individual.

Assessing the right skill of an individual:

The capabilities and the limitations of an individual should be known to him e.g., a person may have interest in painting but may not have the skill to take it as a career. So here the work of vocational guidance comes to assist the individual in assessing himself and then accordingly choosing the right kind of job.

Expansion of the world of work:

Now-a-days jobs are available at national as well as international levels. And it gives rise to many queries as how one can choose the best from several alternatives? How to know about the details of the occupation? How to apply? And many more all these are dealt with the help of vocational guidance.

Functions of Vocational Guidance

Assessment of the individual in terms of his academic achievement, skills attitude, interest, and imitations etc.

Assessment of individual's present environment such as financial resources, family background and family expectations etc.

Assessing the suitability of the individual with that of the job demands. Helping the individual to come at par with the job requirements. Counselling for the adjustment in the job.

Follow-up services in the form of feedback from the individuals for further modification in the guidance programme if needed.

Factors affecting career selection

Aptitudes - What natural abilities do you possess?

Interests - what gives you satisfaction?

Your personality - Do you perform best in low-pressure or high-pressure working environments?

Social Influences on Career Opportunities

Demographic trends

(i) Increase in working parents means more demand for food service and child care.
(ii) More leisure time means more interest in health, and recreation products and services.
(iii) Increased demand for further employment training creates opportunities for teachers and trainers.

Geographic trends

(i) Where jobs are, salaries, and living costs.

(ii) Economic Conditions affect career opportunities

Trends in Industry and Technology affect career opportunities

Automated production methods have decreased the need for many entry-level employees in factories.

Approaches to Career Guidance

Career guidance refers to services and activities which assist individuals, of any age and at any point throughout their lives, to make educational, training and occupational choices and to manage their careers. Such services may be found in schools, universities and colleges, in the workplace. It may take place individually or in group, and may be face-to-face or at a distance. It include career information provision (in print, ICT—based and other forms), assessment and self-assessment tools, counselling interviews, career education programmes.Guidance workers often encounter individuals having very little idea about the skills which they have and the career related to the skill. Sometimes, sufficient time devoted to the early stages of an interview, finding out about the individual.

Others are facial expression, especially glints in the eyes, can be used to know levels of interest in particular types of work. Often, the client will be interested in more than one. Individual judgment is required to look at likely interactions between traits, and selecting the appropriate one.

Holland's Theory of Career Development

The Holland Codes represents a set of personality types described in a theory of careers and vocational choice formulated by psychologist *John L. Holland.* Holland's theory argued that "the choice of a vocation is an expression of personality" and that the six factor typology he articulated could be used to describe both persons and work environments. His model has been adopted by the US. Department of Labor for categorizing jobs relative to interests. The Holland Codes are usually referred to by their first letters: RIASEC.

He presents his theory graphically as hexagon. The shorter the distance between their corners on the hexagon, the more closely they are related. Holland's (1992), theory of career guidance is based on four basic assumptions. The first assumption is that most people can be characterized as one or a combination of six personality types. Second, the theory assumes that the work environment can be classified into the same six categories of personality. Third the theory assumes that people seek out environments compatible with their personality types. And, fourth, the theory holds that particular behavioral patterns emitted in any environment are determined by personality and environmental types. The six personality and work environment types described by Holland are as follows:

(a) ***Realistic:*** Working with your hands, tools, machines, and things; practical, mechanically inclined, and physical. viz., agriculture, computer engineer, basketball player, chef, gardner, martial arts, pilot etc.

(b) ***Investigative:*** Working with theory and information, analytical, intellectual, and scientific, viz., lawyer, statistician, surgeon.

(c) ***Artistic:*** Non-conforming, original, independent, chaotic, creative, viz., actor, writer, and dancer.
(d) ***Social:*** Co-operative environments, supporting, helping, healing/nurturing, viz., psychologist, professor, social worker, and physician.
(e) ***Enterprising:*** Competitive environments, leadership, persuading, viz., public relation, administration, journalism, marketing, and management.
(f) ***Conventional:*** Detail-oriented, organizing, clerical, viz., proof-reader, copy-editing, clerk, and librarian.

Burn Out and Career Guidance

Meaning of Burn out

First let us discuss about the concept of burnout. What is the meaning of the term burn out? Burn out is a psychological term for the experience of long-term exhaustion and diminished interest. It should not be looked as a disorder but as problems related to life-management difficulty. The most well-studied measurement of burnout in the literature is the *Maslach Burnout Inventory. Maslach* and her colleague Jackson first identified the construct "burn out" in the 1970s, and developed a measure that weighs the effects of emotional exhaustion and reduced sense of personal accomplishment. This indicator has become the standard tool for measuring burnout in research on the syndrome. The Maslach Burnout Inventory uses a three dimensional description of exhaustion, cynicism and inefficacy.

Many theories of burnout include negative outcomes related to burnout, including job function, health related outcomes, and mental health problems. The term burnout in psychology was coined by *Herbert Freudenberger* in *1974. Psychologists Herbert Freudenberger and Gail North* gave 12 phases of burnout, which are not necessarily followed sequentially:

A compulsion to prove oneself; working harder; Neglecting one's own needs; Displacement of conflicts (the person does not realize the root cause of the distress); Revision of values (friends or hobbies are completely dismissed); Renial of emerging problems (cynicism and aggression become apparent); withdrawal (reducing social contacts to a minimum, becoming walled off; alcohol or other substance abuse may occur); Behavioral changes become obvious to others; Depersonalisation (life becomes a series of mechanical functions); Inner emptiness; Depression; Burnout syndrome.

The signs can vary from individual to individual, but the following are some universal indicators that one can use to determine if career burnout is occurring.

(a) ***Depression*:** Feelings of despair and sadness that last for weeks or months usually signal that something in your life is not working like it should and is cause for an investigation into the cause – potentially your job.

(b) ***Lack of energy:*** If individual experience constant fatigue throughout the day.

(c) ***Lack of desire:*** If an individual find that he just don't care if he is successful or not it's a warning that the individual may have become burned out.

(d) ***Decreased productivity:*** If the productivity of an individual is decreased and he is not coming upto the desired expected result.

(e) ***Increased absences and/or tardiness:*** If an individual finds every opportunity to skip out on work.

(f) ***Boredom:*** Occasional boredom in one's career is completely normal; however, pervasive feelings of weariness and dreariness are not and are an indicator of potential burnout.

(g) ***Anger/resentment in workplace:*** Frequently lashing out at coworkers and/or supervisors is unacceptable under any circumstance. This behavior deserves immediate attention due to its potentially abusive nature.

(h) ***Sleep problems:*** Insomnia or occasional fatigue can happen to anyone but are a cause for concern if they become constant and a part of your everyday life. Sleep disturbances are your body's way of saying it is overworked.

Coping with Burnout

There is variety of ways that both individuals and organizations can deal with burnout. In his book, Managing stress: Emotion and power at work (1995), Newton argues that many of the remedies related to burnout are motivated not from an employee's perspective, but from the organisation's perspective. Let us now discuss some of the common strategies for dealing with burnout.

Organisational aspects

Employee assistance programs (EAP): Employee Assistance Programs were designed to assist employees in dealing with the primary causes of stress. Some programs included counselling and psychological services for employees. But nowadays it is less utilised as compared to stress management training (SMT).

Stress management training (SMT): Stress Management Training (SMT) is employed by many organisations today as a way to get employees to either work through stress or to manage their stress levels.

Individual aspects

Problem-based coping-Individual can cope with the problems related to burnout and stress by focusing on the causes of the stress. This type of coping has successfully been linked to reductions in individual stress.

Appraisal-based coping-Appraisal-based coping strategies deal with individual interpretations of what is and is not a stress inducing activity.

6

Social Counselling and Guidance

Numerous definitions of counselling exist, but one of the more succinct and helpful descriptions are that by Burks and Stefflre:

"Counselling denotes a professional relationship between a trained counsellor and a client. This relationship is usually person-to-person, although it may sometimes involve more than two people. It is designed to help clients understand and clarify their views on their life space, and to learn to reach their self-determined goals through meaningful, well-informed choices and through resolution of problems of an emotional or interpersonal nature."

Counselling may focus on both work-related and personal problems, which can include coping with crisis, conflict with others, development of personal insights and improving relationships. Sessions usually last for between 50 and 60 minutes and take place within a confidential setting. Frequency and duration varies, depending on the client's needs, availability and the model of counselling employed. Traditionally, counseling happens face-to-face but alternatives—such as telephone, video-conferencing and online counselling - have emerged in recent years.

Counselling is increasingly recognised as a specific professional discipline, as distinct from the use of counseling skills, which are employed routinely by most health service professionals in the course of their work. It is likely that the area of psychological therapies will become legally regulated within the next few years, with titles such as 'counsellor' and 'psychotherapist' being protected.

The minimum level of training that is generally recognised by the professional bodies for counselling and psychotherapy is a diploma, which includes both theory and practice components. Here are some of the main requirements of professional counselling practice.

Accountability

(i) Counsellors should be properly trained and experienced for the work they carry out.
(ii) They should belong to a recognised professional body, with a code of professional practice and a complaints procedure.
(iii) Clinical supervision is vital and counsellors should receive at least the minimum level required by their professional body.

Responsibility

(i) The primary focus of the counselling is the needs of the client.
(ii) Counsellors should avoid situations that give rise to conflicts of interest between their responsibilities to their clients and other parties. This usually means they do not have any other role with their clients.
(iii) Counselling takes place in an appropriate setting that ensures the confidentiality of the relationship between the client and the counsellor.

Workplace Counselling

Workplace counselling is a specialised field, whereby the employer either provides a service or access to one. Over the last decade it has become one of the fastest growing fields within counselling. Most of the growth has taken place in the private rather than public sector, with many large corporate companies now offering this service.

In most cases, the health service has been slower to recognise the benefits for its staff, but in many areas this protected. Counselling for staff can either be provided internally through a service located in the organisation and by staff employed by the organisation — or externally, where an external provider is contracted to provide the service. Wherever, the service is located, the issue of accountability for counsellors can be complex.

This may be to either the employer or to an intermediate provider, depending on whether the service is provided internally or contracted out. In addition, legal, commercial and health and safety considerations may impinge on the counseling relationship. Given these complex factors, it is recommended that newly qualified counsellors should not be employed in these settings unless they can be adequately supported and that, ideally, counsellors should have a minimum of three years' post qualification experience.

Staff perceptions of the service's confidentiality are crucial and if employees remain unconvinced, it will not gain the trust necessary to succeed. Whether provided internally or externally, the boundaries between counselling and other functions — such as human resources and occupational health — should be clearly defined. Occasionally staff may be involved in disciplinary processes at work and use the counselling service for support.

However, counselling as described within this guidance should not form part of or be confused with any disciplinary process. Counselling should only be undertaken voluntarily and staff should not be coerced into using the service. Managers and colleagues acting out of concern may suggest contact with a counselling service, but essentially staff should self-refer, free of pressure.

Managers should also be sensitive to the needs of staff using the service, for example in enabling them to use the service during work time, and also respect their right to confidentiality.

The following points identify some of the principle features of counselling practice as it applies to the workplace:

(i) Most counselling provision is short-term, with services offering between six and eight sessions, including an initial assessment;
(ii) In addition to the minimum professional level qualification of a diploma, counsellors need to be able to work within a short-term counselling framework;

(iii) Counsellors work with an understanding of the organizational culture—in this case the health service; —and of organisational factors which impact on psychological health in the workplace;

(iv) Counsellors work with an awareness of the interests of different organisational stakeholders and of the potential for conflicts of interest between the needs of the client, the service and other stakeholders.

A range of evidence exists supporting the idea that workplace counselling helps to reduce the level of psychological distress in staff, improves work functioning and lowers absenteeism. For example, the *British Association for Counselling and Psychotherapy* commissioned a rigorous and independent research review of the evidence to date into the effectiveness of workplace counselling. The results are important pointers to some of the successes within the field of workplace counselling.

Individuals can refer themselves to psychological support at a time of crisis and distress. Acknowledgement of a problem can be the psychological turning point for the individual. Many staff wait too long before accessing help and the availability of immediate psychological support can reduce distress, helping the individual maintain their role at work.

The Mc Leod study found strong evidence of the individual benefit from workplace counselling, concluding that: "People who make use of workplace counselling typically report high levels of psychological distress, equivalent to that found in out-patient psychiatric populations, Significant benefits for clients can be achieved in three to eight sessions of counselling; only the most severely disturbed clients appear to require long-term counseling help or referral to a specialist service...Counselling interventions are generally effective in alleviating symptoms of anxiety, stress, and depression. Two-thirds of studies have shown that, following counselling, levels of work-related symptoms and stress return to the normal range for more than 50 per cent of clients."

The study by Leeds and Sheffield Universities evaluated two NHS trust staff counselling services, finding a significant reduction in the proportion of clients with significant levels of psychological disturbance. And a study by Cary Cooper into counselling provision in the Post Office found marked reductions in symptoms of depression and anxiety, as well as significant organisational benefits. It is also clear that counselling at work is well received by staff. McLeod states that: "Over 90 per cent of employees who make use of workplace counselling are highly satisfied with the service they have received, would use it again if necessary, and would recommend it to colleagues."

Benefits

The McLeod review also found evidence of very considerable benefits for organisations in having counselling provision. The study concluded that: "Counselling interventions have been found, in the majority of studies to have reduced sickness absence rates in clients by 25-50 per cent. Counselling interventions have a lesser, but still significant, positive impact on job commitment, work function, job satisfaction and substance misuse." The study by Cooper into the Post Office's counselling provision also found evidence of considerable organisational benefits. Cooper found substantial reductions in absence; duration of absence for the six months pre- and post-counselling; reductions in use of other human resources and in frequency and duration of authorised absence; and disciplinary proceedings.

Smewing, in a study of a NHS-based Employee Assistance Programme (EAP), found that even staff that had not used the counselling service felt more valued by the organisation, which led to a 'feel good' factor about their employer.

Cost issues are important because counselling provision for staff is essentially competing for resources with other priorities. The more effectively it can demonstrate its value, the more successful it is likely to be in attracting resources. In addition to the Lothian study already cited, *McLeod examined* a range of studies looking at the cost effectiveness of workplace counseling and EAP provision. His conclusion is that: "Even the most rigorous economic analyses show that workplace counselling and EAPs cover their costs, in terms of economic savings that are generated by employers."

There is strong evidence that counselling has a positive impact on organisational health and a properly targetted intervention will at least pay for itself. However, not all counseling interventions are equally effective and clearly there is a link between service quality and outcomes. Service evaluation is crucial in determining the effectiveness of individual services and how it may be enhanced.

Currently, access to counselling for staff in the health service is far from universal and, where it is provided, is extremely varied in its range and quality. Provision ranges from single – and often part-time – counsellors engaged for limited hours and providing only counselling, to well-resourced services employing a number of staff and providing a range of additional services. The majority of services appear to be either internally provided, or purchased on a contract basis from other health services providers who already have internal provision.

Given that health care is delivered in a range of widely differing settings and by a range of professional and support staff, the manner in which counselling is provided will inevitably need to reflect this. However, in UK, the Royal College of Nursing (RCN) believes that there are some core elements of service provision that should be available for all staff. Counselling is currently provided in two main ways, either face-to-face or by telephone.

Most of the staffs prefer to see a counsellor in person and this should be an essential part of the service provision. However, this may be difficult to provide – for example, where staffs are working in remote locations – and in these situations, telephone counselling may be appropriate. The key principle is to ensure that all staff can refer themselves to a quality service. While most services usually offer between six and eight sessions, there should be the option of additional sessions where the counselor makes a clinical judgement that the client needs extra support.

Counsellors should be trained or experienced in short-term work. The service should have links with local mental health services and other agencies to enable referral where needed.

Traumatic incidents

Traumatic incidents may include physical or verbal assault, a drug error, involvement in a critical incident inquiry - for example, suicide or homicide - or witnessing a fatal accident. It is quite common for staff, who have been exposed to traumatic incidents to develop a range of reactions and post-trauma symptoms, some of which may be distressing and disabling. Both in the short and longer term, the individual's well-being and performance may be severely affected.

Most symptoms generally diminish over a few weeks, but where they persist they may indicate the presence of *Post Traumatic Stress Disorder* (PTSD) or another psychological disorder. While only a small proportion of staff exposed to critical incidents develops PTSD, support following a traumatic incident at work should be available to all staff. Although this is a specialist area of work, which requires appropriate training, staff counselling services are in a good position to provide post incident support.

In addition, psychological debriefing should not be set-up in isolation — the Department of Health's Treatment Choice in Psychological Therapies and Counselling states that it should only be employed where follow-up and access to other psychological support is available, for example, a staff counselling service.

Framework services

The way in which services are established is critical to their success. To ensure that services fulfill their potential, careful consideration of their purpose, structure and resourcing is required. Central to establishing a successful service is organisational ownership and the involvement of key stakeholders.

A development or advisory group can help to ensure that the interests of the various stakeholders are taken into account. This should include senior management - for example the director of nursing or human resources - and the views of staff and unions, with their active involvement if possible, enabling users to have confidence in their service.

The broad aims of the service should be informed by human resource issues - like levels of stress and sickness absence, staff attitude surveys and critical incident records - but they must be realistic. For example, don't assume that establishing a counseling service will result in an immediate fall in sickness absence or reduce the threat of litigation. These can only be achieved if counselling is offered as part of a wider organisational response, specifically addressing the work factors that give rise to these concerns.

More achievable aims might include:

(i) Providing timely psychological support to staff experiencing stress or distress, preventing further deterioration of symptoms and an adverse impact on work performance;
(ii) Contributing to the return to work of staff whose psychological health has resulted in absence from work;
(iii) Effectively, managing critical incidents and providing appropriate support to staff affected.

The key objectives and functions of the service can be determined from the overall aims. Objective setting is important in that it provides the subsequent basis for evaluating the overall effectiveness of the service. Objectives will be specific to each organisation but should capture the contribution that services can make to staff as clients and to the wider organisation. Here are some examples:

(i) Providing professional, short-term, confidential counselling to all staff;
(ii) Providing counselling, both face-to-face and by telephone;
(iii) offering training and consultancy to managers to help staff who are experiencing distress;
(iv) Providing post incident support to staff, including debriefing as appropriate;
(v) Contributing to organisational policy and practice in critical incident management.

Additional service objectives or functions may also be identified, for example:

(i) Providing training for staff in counselling and communication skills, managing stress and psychological responses to traumatic situations;

(ii) Offering mediation or conflict resolution giving careers advice;

Both internal and external models of service delivery have their benefits and problems and a number of issues need to be considered before making a choice. These include the size of the organisation and whether it can sustain its own provision, or whether it would be better to contract with an external provider with an existing service. Geographical area may be a deciding factor and, if an external private provider is selected, you will need to ascertain whether it can provide what it claims.

However, the service is provided, it should be based on a set of clear quality criteria that form the basis for monitoring and evaluating its quality and effectiveness. In terms of staff as clients, it can be important that they feel the counsellor understands the nature of their role within the organisation. Through its understanding of the organisation, the service can be highly responsive to need and also contribute to and inform the wider human resource agenda by, for example, advising on the management of major organisational change.

Clinical supervision of the work of counsellors is normally external and this is considered good practice in most workplace and other organisational settings. Provided the service is of a sufficient size, a service manager who is experienced in workplace counselling can be appointed to have responsibility for the clinical work of the service. The service needs to be located so as to protect the confidentiality of service users. Where the organisation covers a wide geographical area or is delivered from a range of different locations, thought should be given to ensuring that staffs are able to access the service easily.

The appropriate level of resourcing for services will depend on a range of factors, including the size of the organisation, the anticipated uptake by staff, and the functions that the service is expected to provide. In UK, NHS Executive guidance suggests a ratio of one full-time counsellor per 2,000 staff, where counsellors have no role other than counselling, and where they work from a single site. More staff may be needed if the service fulfils additional functions or operates from different sites.

An alternative model for assessing the level of counselling resources required can be based on anticipated staff uptake and the optimum caseload capacity of counsellors. While usage cannot be predicted in advance, studies of workplace counselling provision suggest that an assumption that up to ten per cent of staff may use the service in any one year is not unreasonable.

Broadly, there are two models within the health service—the first being NHS-based workplace counselling services. These are located in one organisation, but also provide services to neighbouring trusts and other employers. This model tends to be the most popular amongst health service organisations without their own service. The second is the large number of commercial providers that offer a range of counselling and other services, usually known as Employee Assistance Programmes (EAPs).

They mainly work off-site and their counsellors (sometimes called associates) are usually self-employed and may work for a number of EAP providers. External provision may be appropriate for smaller organisations that cannot sustain their own internal provision, or where the organisation simply wants to provide counselling and nothing else. Larger EAPs cover a wide geographical area, offer twenty four-hour access to services and can provide a range of additional services, such as critical incident support and legal and debt advice.

NHS-based providers will have a good understanding of the health service context and experience in delivering counseling to health service staff.

Depending on how important this is to the purchasing organisation, this could form part of the specification.

EAP providers may offer very comprehensive packages that the organisation does not require. One of the limitations of external provision is a lack of direct control over quality.

A clear system for reporting of service activity should be established at the outset. Reporting should enable the organisation to determine whether the service is achieving its aims and deal with any resource issues that may arise. The process should also seek to identify areas of concern that may need to be examined by the wider organisation, for example, a high proportion of service users experiencing bullying and harassment.

Counselling Services and their Role in Wider Staff Support and Organisational Culture

Services that are purely reactive, only providing counselling for distressed employees, miss an important opportunity to help create a healthier organisation. For example, organisational change is now increasingly commonplace within the health service and is one area where staff counselling services can make a vital contribution.

Services routinely work with clients who are affected by victims of poorly managed change. They have a valuable role to play in discussions at management or board level about how proposed changes may impact operationally and the best way to implement them. Many organisations fail to recognise this contribution and need time to embrace this new way of working.

If counselling services are provided internally, experience shows that most will need to be established for between two and three years before their role and functions are fully understood and they are able to contribute to the wider organisation.

There are a number of basic prerequisites for a successful integrated service. The organisation needs to recognise the potential contribution services can make to both individual staff and the wider organisation. The service needs to maintain its profile within the organisation and seek opportunities for contributing to the organisational agenda.

It requires counsellors who are comfortable about operating in an organisational context and can manage any tensions that may arise in meeting the needs of both the client and the organisation. Most counselling and staff support services within health service settings, particularly those that are more established and integrated, offer a range of additional services that contribute to a more comprehensive model of employee support, with overall staff well-being at their core.

Services have an important role to play in *destigmatising* issues of psychological distress. This may include educating others about coping with stress or understanding the psychological effects of trauma. Services can also provide training on issues like managing distressed staff, counselling skills and handling stress. This kind of educational activity provides opportunities for staff to meet counsellors in a different capacity, raising the profile of the service.

Providing confidential and objective career guidance through workplace counselling services can reap enormous benefits for both the individual and the organisation. Supporting staff to make career decisions helps to ensure a more motivated work force and will ultimately increase retention rates. Services provided by career advisers include support with job applications and interview techniques, feedback on self-awareness exercises and psychometric tests, guidance on educational and career options in the health service, support with personal development planning and access to a range of career resources.

Financial problems can impact on other aspects of life and, if not dealt with early, can have devastating results, even leading to the loss of a home. A pre-occupation with financial difficulties can easily spill over into the work place and giving staff the opportunity to talk to an independent adviser, in confidence, can alleviate some of the stress and provide practical options for dealing with debt. At a minimum, services should have a list of resources for local debt advice, although in some areas arranging an appointment can take several weeks.

The counselling service should establish effective good links with the local statutory and voluntary sector mental health services to enable referral to alternative or additional sources of psychological or practical support. These may include other counselling and psychotherapy services, Citizens Advice Bureaux, law centres and other agencies that offer support, such as GP practices and unions. Development of these links should be considered from the outset.

From an employer's perspective, the rationale for providing staff counselling is likely to be to improve psychological well-being, performance and attendance. All services should try to determine how effective counselling is in achieving these aims. Audit and evaluation should be integrated into service planning and development, ideally incorporating three key areas:

(i) Routine audit of service utilization,
(ii) Routine audit of aspects of service quality, including effectiveness,
(iii) The overall objectives of the service.

Routine audit and evaluation are likely to inform the broader question of whether the service is meeting its overall objectives, helping to determine whether they remain realistic or need revision. Depending on the objectives of the service, some specific measures of effectiveness may be required. For example, if one of the service's objectives is helping staff suffering from stress to return to work, measures of pre and post counseling, absence or work functioning will be required. Functions that are offered in addition to counselling may need their own individual evaluation frameworks.

The measurement of service utilisation, quality and effectiveness varies widely across psychological therapy services generally and workplace counselling is no exception. Most services routinely audit service utilisation and some seek client feedback on their experience of the service. A relatively small number have attempted to quantify the outcomes of counselling for their clients. Many of the measurement tools currently in use have been developed by individual services, with only a few appearing to use valid and reliable measures to evaluate effectiveness.

While these 'home grown' systems undoubtedly yield valuable data, their drawback is that they offer no opportunity for comparing data with other services and no possibility of determining whether the data is representative of the wider workplace counselling sector. The RCN's counselling service has been using a standardised system since March 1999. The *CORE (Clinical Outcomes in Routine Evaluation)* system is the first in the UK to apply audit, evaluation and outcome measurement to counselling and psychological therapy settings.

The RCN has been collaborating with the Psychological Therapies Research Centre and other partners to adapt CORE to the needs of workplace counselling, and has been part of a collaborative research project involving seven workplace counselling services using the CORE system. The findings of this research project build on the conclusions of the McLeod study that workplace counselling is highly effective. The study found that the psychological health profile of staff using counselling services is almost identical to that of clients using primary care counselling, and that workplace counselling has the potential to:

(i) improve mental health for 78 per cent of clients;
(ii) reduce rates of sickness and absence;
(iii) enhance work functioning.

Adolescents, who constitute over one-fifth of India's population, have limited access to vital information and services pertaining to sexual and reproductive health (SRH). Cultural taboos surrounding communication about sexual matters persist in the parent-child relationship, and young people have few opportunities outside their peer group to talk about their feelings and anxieties.

Founded in 1949, the *Family Planning Association of India (FPAI)* is the country's largest *nongovernmental organisation (NGO)* providing family planning and other reproductive health services.

In addition to clinical services, training and research, FPAI carries out extensive information, education and communications programmes throughout India. The FPAI has experimented with numerous programmes to meet the needs of both urban and rural youth, including campaigns to increase the age at marriage, sexuality and reproductive health education programmes, and counselling services.

In the late 1960s, FPAI began educating young people in schools, colleges and non-formal educational institutions on issues related to population and family life. These programmes provide an orientation for young people regarding sexuality, reproductive health, the prevention of unplanned pregnancies and sexually transmitted infections (STIs). In designing these programmes, the FPAI kept in view that adolescents have needs that are distinct from those of adults. These education programmes do not merely provide information, but also aim to enhance young people's communication skills, clarify values, change attitudes and prevent risky behaviour.

In 1978, FPAI established Sexuality Education Counselling Research Therapy/Training (SECRT) centres, which provide sexuality education and counselling. Today 37 SECRT centres have reached over 120,000 young people. SECRT centres offer counselling services to both married and unmarried adults and adolescents, on a range of topics, including premarital counselling, family planning and marital and infertility counselling.

FPAI offers these services individually, in groups, by correspondence and over the telephone. FPAI has developed several innovative approaches in partnership with young people to promote sexual and reproductive health. The organisation works through youth clubs in many settings to provide accurate information on family life and adolescent health matters, including the prevention of sexually transmitted infections, including human Immmuno Deficiency Virus Infection (STIs/HIV).

In addition, FPAI branches have developed peer educator initiatives in collaboration with other youth programmes, such as Youth Parliament, Young Women Information Centres and thespian programmes. In addition, FPAI has developed "Young Inspirers Clubs" in rural and urban areas. These clubs use folk media to raise awareness about STIs/ HIV/AIDS, to eradicate myths and misconceptions related to sexuality, and to promote reproductive health.

In 1997, FPAI-SECRT initiated "Spearhead Youth Health Leadership Training Programme". This programme has trained nearly 1000 youth leaders, many of whom have served as peer counsellors in the FPAI Young Inspirers Clubs. In 1999, the FPAI implemented a project on "Enhancing Sexual and Reproductive Health of Young Persons". This project aimed to extend information and counselling on issues related to human sexuality, preparation for marriage, responsible parenthood, gender issues, contraception and prevention of STIs/HIV/AIDS. As part of the project, the six FPAI branches carried out sensitisation programmes, organised medical check-up camps and provided counselling and training for teachers and peer educators. The project reached out to rural and urban youth, and the response was overwhelming.

For example, the STI/HIV prevention programme reached 7065 young people, including 3391 out-of-school, illiterate youth. In Dharwad (Karnataka), the project established a strong network of young people trained to impart knowledge on sexuality and STIs/ HIV/AIDS. Its peer group leaders' training led to the establishment of eight community counselling centres in six villages where four to five peer group leaders provide counselling on a regular basis.

Psychological and Social Needs of Parents

"Support" is defined as including all activities or arrangements within the health-care environment which help meet the psychological and social needs of parents whose children are receiving care, whether or not they are specifically intended to fulfill this purpose. Support thus covers a wide range of issues from practical arrangements for parents to stay in the hospital and help in their children's care to the giving of information, encouragement, advice and sympathy. It follows that anyone involved in the provision or organisation of care at an individual or institutional level may have a part to play in ensuring that parents' needs are provided for and taken into account. Support may also be provided from sources outside the health care setting including self-help groups or facilitator-led support groups.

Within the broader framework of psychological and social support, counselling is the activity which occurs when a person (either regularly or temporarily in the role of counsellor) offers time, attention and respect to another person or persons to explore their feelings and concerns. Counselling has been defined by Bor *et al* as:

"An interaction in a therapeutic setting, focusing primarily on a conversation about relationships, beliefs and behaviour (including feelings), through which the patient's perceived problem is elucidated and framed or reframed in a fitting or useful way, and in which new solutions are generated and the problem takes on a new meaning."

There are four different levels of counselling in health care settings:

(i) ***Information-giving:*** The provision of factual information and advice about medical conditions, laboratory tests, treatments etc.
(ii) ***Implications counselling:*** A discussion with the patient and/or others which addresses the implications of the information for the individual or family and their personal circumstances.
(iii) ***Supportive counselling:*** In which the emotional consequences of the information and its implications can be identified and addressed in a supportive and caring environment.
(iv) ***Psychotherapeutic counselling*:** Focusses on healing, psychological adjustment, coping and problem resolution.

The first two levels are likely to be regarded as a routine part of care for all patients, which will usually be provided by the health professionals responsible for their medical and nursing care. In certain situations (such as bereavement and diagnostic testing for genetic disorders or HIV) where psychological issues are recognised as particularly significant, supportive counselling may also be offered to all patients. Formal psychotherapeutic counselling will not be needed by all patients and is more likely to be provided through referral to a specialist counsellor.

Counselling skills, such as listening, reflecting and conveying empathy, are not exclusive to the counsellor. Almost all health care professionals need such skills in the course of their interactions with patients, for example in giving information, clarifying treatment options and helping people adjust to new and sometimes unwelcome circumstances. The difference between these generic skills and those of a formally defined counsellor (or psychologist or psychotherapist) is that the latter is expected to have advanced training and qualifications in their field and is likely to approach the counselling process within a specific theoretical framework (such as humanistic counselling, psychodynamic counselling or cognitive behaviour counselling).

Families may present a number of times for therapy, each time with different needs and dilemmas with only minimal contact in between. Formal counselling interventions for families of children who are sick vary according to the task faced by the family. Examples include crisis counselling to help facilitate and contain emotional expression following diagnosis or relapse; insight-orientated psychotherapy for considering future uncertainty over illness; and family therapy when unacknowledged conflict, or differing opinion on appropriate coping strategies and communication, is resulting in problems such as non-compliance with therapies or refusing to eat.

Some of the problems experienced by parents are caused simply by being with their children in an unfamiliar institutional setting and are not specific to the hospital context or the child's illness or treatment. Other difficulties derive from the way in which hospitals in particular are organised and the role that parents are expected to play in their child's care. Others again reflect the inherent anxieties associated with serious illness and vary according to the circumstances of the individual child.

Problems of being in a strange environment include:

Lack of familiarity: Not knowing the way around, who is who, who does what, where and when to ask for information, how and when things happen, what to expect or what is expected of oneself.

Isolation: From usual resources, social networks and one's own usual social roles.

The ordinary care of any child involves meeting his or her physical, psychological, social and spiritual needs. These are normally met primarily by the family. Illness affects the nature of some or all of these needs, and also the ability of the family to meet them. Hospitalisation of a child forces changes in the parents' view of themselves as protectors and nurturers. They may have to relinquish much of their parenting role to the nurses, being anxious about performing even normal every day care on a sick child in an unfamiliar environment and not knowing what they are expected or permitted to do.

Parent's views about the amount of involvement they would like to have in their child's care vary and the same parents' views may change over time as their own and their child's circumstances alter. It is suggested that the best way of achieving an appropriate balance of care is through negotiation between nursing staff and individual families to reach agreement-based on the parents' wishes rather than by imposing the expectations of the professional staff.

Participation is desired by parents and children and is also consistent with current discourse about empowerment and involvement of users in health-care. Nevertheless, such involvement may exacerbate some of the financial, social and personal costs experienced by parents:

Financial costs may include: costs of travelling to hospital, especially where children are being treated in regional centres; extra costs of staying away from home (buying meals, telephones, paying for alternative care for siblings); loss of income (especially for those who are self-employed).

***Social costs may include*:** Using up holiday entitlement; depleting reserves of goodwill from employers, friends or neighbours who may be co-opted in to help Personal costs. Participation in unpleasant experiences (such as accompanying a child to the anaesthetic room, staying with them during a painful procedure or refusing to let them have a drink) has been identified as difficult because it challenges parents' ideas of themselves and their usual roles in providing for or protecting their children. This may be seen by parents and staff as something to be coped with, rather than avoided, because of the benefits to both child and parent of having the parent present and involved.

Suggested strategies for limiting some of the costs of parental involvement include:

(i) Ensuring that parental costs are taken into account in the design of services (*e.g.*, by ensuring parents are not expected to pay more than hospital workers for food and drink).
(ii) Enabling parents to choose whether or not to participate in their child's care and not to be required to be involved simply because of lack of nursing staff.

For all parents of children with serious illness, one of the most important sources of stress will be anxiety about the child itself and its condition. In a study of mothers whose children had been admitted unexpectedly to a paediatric intensive care unit, respondents described the sudden transition from having a healthy child to having a child who was critically ill as causing catastrophic feelings of shock, guilt, helplessness and confusion.

Key issues identified included

(i) The tension experienced while getting to and waiting for their partners to reach the hospital;
(ii) Waiting in acute stress without nursing assessment or therapeutic support through a period of enforced separation during the medical stabilisation of the child being re-united with a child whose appearance had changed (being nursed naked, intubated, ventilated and attached to a variety of monitors and infusion devices).

A study of the experiences of parents whose children suffered neurological damage after cardiac surgery identified the following:

(i) Shock, loss and grief, combined for some parents with a profound sense of "aloneness";

(ii) Guilt, blame and anger - almost all the parents identified a specific focus of blame for their child's brain damage. These included "medicine", "the driver", "the child" and "themselves";
(iii) Fear for the own sanity linked to emotional and physical exhaustion;
(iv) Fear of injuring the disabled child and thoughts of euthanasia.

The death of a child has been repeatedly identified as the most traumatic experience a family will endure. The grief process has been described as falling into three phases: a period of numbness, shock, disbelief and unreality; a period of intense grief; and a period of reorganisation and recovery. Additional feelings that may arise include anger, helplessness, rage, frustration and guilt. Behavioural reactions to these feelings can include hysteria, crying, wailing, hitting and physical acting out. Aspects of emotional support that have been found to be helpful to families after the death of a child in hospital include: listening, talking openly and honestly, providing words of comfort, showing feelings, providing privacy and choosing words carefully.

In a paediatric intensive care unit, families may be exposed to deaths of children other than their own. On such units, families often form their own support network and become important parts of each other's "family" while their children are ill.

Witnessing the death of someone else's child in the unit will intensify fears of death and feelings of uncertainty about one's own child's outcome.

Watching a child die, especially, if witnessed more than once, may also cast doubts on the belief that one's own child is receiving the best care possible. For all these reasons, it is suggested that parents present during and after the death of a child other than their own have significant needs and their normal coping behaviours may be compromised if they feel their needs are insignificant compared with those of the bereaved family.

Waiting has been identified as one of the most stressful parts of the experience for parents of hospitalised children. Remaining inactive and unable to leave an area for fear of missing an important report denies an individual the mobility often used to deal with stress and can lead to feelings of powerlessness. Families who wait often feel neglected and forgotten. The expected event — a test result, a date for surgery or an improvement in the child's condition — is often unpredictable and uncertain. All of these characteristics may affect the parent's ability to cope with the stress of waiting.

Manifestations of waiting when the outcome is not known include fear, fatigue, anxiety, lack of ability to concentrate, restlessness, inability to eat or drink, anger and frustration.

Stressful periods of waiting occur at various different stages in the child's care. These include waiting:

(i) For admission, for surgery and for discharge (all of which may be unexpectedly brought forward or postponed for a variety of reasons not always directly connected with the child involved);
(ii) For the results of diagnostic tests (to know what is wrong and what the prognosis and required treatment may be);
(iii) During surgery and medical treatment (waiting to know whether the child has come through alright and whether the treatment has been successful);

Some waiting is unavoidable (*i.e.*, that related to the time it takes to perform tests, procedures and surgery and for a child's condition to improve). Other types of waiting could potentially be reduced or eliminated (that relating to admissions procedures, pain alleviation, delay in conveying medical reports and messages and arrival in a treatment area long before the procedure can be done). Following strategies to help parents cope with waiting include:

(i) Acknowledge to parents that it is difficult to wait;
(ii) Provide a comfortable setting in which to wait;
(iii) Assist parents to find a support person to share the waiting;
(iv) Be aware of parents' physical needs (for food etc.,) while they wait;
(v) Keep parents regularly informed of progress;
(vi) Ensure a system for prompt delivery of messages;

(vii) Assist parents to use coping strategies that have helped them before;
(vii) Use hospital volunteers to maintain waiting areas and help meet parents' needs;
(viii) Develop strategies for care delivery that minimise avoidable waiting.

Parental Stress

Stress among parents of children admitted to paediatric intensive-care units found that:

(i) Parents' experiencing unexpected admission of their child had higher stress scores on all dimensions than planned admission parents;
(ii) Parents' overall stress levels are the highest early on in the experience of hospitalisation and diminish over time (except where things go wrong);
(iii) Factors concerning the child (diagnosis, prognosis, experience of pain) and the parents' relationship with their child were major sources of stress and were more important to parents than factors affecting their own comfort, self-care or spiritual needs;

Several studies have been undertaken to identify parents' own perceptions of their needs for support while their children are in hospital. Identified needs include:

(i) To receive accurate information about their child's condition that is honest, exact, understandable, ongoing, freely offered, consistent, well-timed and comprehensive;
(ii) To have ready access to their child, continue in the parental role, have meaningful participation in their care and be recognised as important to their recovery;
(iii) To trust in the staff and feel that they care about (as well as for) the child;
(iv) To be assured that the child is receiving the best care possible;
(v) To receive support from their own social networks (including relatives, friends and workplace colleagues); andopportunities

for the direct involvement of grandparents and siblings (include somewhere for the latter to play);

Needs identified by parents whose children who had suffered brain damage after surgery included:

(i) Contact with other families in similar situations;
(ii) An individual with whom they could build a trusting one-to-one relationship (both at the time of the injury and afterwards) with the skills and detachment to discuss the tragedy openly and to listen to their doubts, anxieties or anger as parents. It was frequently suggested that this person should be detached from the child's care, available on a regular basis and easy to reach as required.
(iii) The provision of written summaries about their child's brain damage, to ease the burden of having to retell the story to every new contact.
(iv) Information about local support services, within the first few weeks, repeated as required and in writing of or the fate and future of children like their own to be openly discussed by society and by the medical profession.

The 1959 Platt Report on the welfare of children in hospital, led to radical changes in, among other things, access and provision for parents. These original government recommendations were based on a psychological view point, but research carried out subsequently added a sociological dimension-based on the relationship between the child and family and the discontinuity in family life caused by hospital admission.Over the past few years; there has been an increasing consensus between government, professional and voluntary organisations on the benefits of parental participation in "family-centred" care.

The 1991 guidance advises the agreement of service specifications which:

(i) Recognise that parents and members of the immediate family are not visitors, encourage and assist them to be with their child at all times (especially those that are most stressful *i.e.*, during anaesthesia, treatments, investigations and during post-operative recovery) and enable them to give continuous love, care, comfort and support to their child.

(ii) Help parents to undertake many familiar tasks helpful to the care of their child and provide help and advice to continue the care following the child's discharge.

It also recommends that hospital routines should be sufficiently flexible to adapt to families' different cultural practices and that parents be encouraged to express their preferences for the care of their children in relation to diet and feeding, clothing, washing and bathing, and beliefs or traditions in respect of healing, treatment and care while dying.

The 1991 guidance encourages health authorities and hospitals to establish links with voluntary organisations active in their areas to achieve maximum co-operation in the planning and organisation of services like social work support. It also recommends that those involved in agreeing contracts should ensure that:

(i) All staff are sensitive to the needs of children and their families with life-threatening conditions and are able to draw upon staff specifically trained in care and counselling.

(ii) Parents are informed in an appropriate manner, as soon as possible of their child's condition and given every opportunity to talk through their feelings.

(iii) Care is taken not to "avoid" parents whose child is dying, while at the same time recognising the need for privacy.

(iv) Where children are taken home, advice is available to parents on the help available from statutory or voluntary agencies to ensure ongoing support and counselling for as long as necessary to parents have the opportunity to return to the hospital to find out anything further they wish to know about any aspect of their child's illness, care or treatment.

When a child dies, the 1991 guidance states that it is essential that parents/carers are helped to cope with the sense of loss and grief and also given practical assistance to help them make necessary decisions. Health authorities and hospitals are advised to ensure that:

(i) A member of staff trained in care and counselling is designated to give families, including siblings, all the necessary support including help with the arrangement of bereavement counselling and practical issues like burial arrangements.
(ii) The results of any post-mortem investigation are conveyed in a sympathetic manner to the family in order that the therapeutic value of the discussion of the pathologist's findings is fully realised.
(iii) The family's GP is informed as soon as possible so that, as necessary, the GP can help them cope with the medical effects of bereavement.

The 1996 Children's Charter contains a number of statements about the rights and expectations of parents whose children are sick. These include rights:

(i) To take part in any discussions and decisions about the child's treatment and care and to be kept up to date with their progress;
(ii) For the child to have a named consultant paediatrician or surgeon and named qualified nurse to look after them and provide quality of care;
(iii) To stay in hospital with the child, participate in their care, accompany them to the anaesthetic room and be informed about pain relief.

In addition to the Department of Health guidance, a number of professional and voluntary bodies have made recommendations in recent years concerning the care of children in hospital. Most of these endorse or reiterate the standards contained in the DOH guidance in relation to parental involvement and support. Some go into more detail about how services should be managed in this respect or make additional recommendations.

A 1995 report by the *British Paediatric Association (BPA)* points up the "vital role" of the specialist social worker. It observes that the combination of social work skills and knowledge of rare and life threatening conditions give them an advantage in dealing with the problems that arise in families when a child has a serious disease or organ failure. It observes that in some regions, specialist social worker posts have been reduced or discontinued because of new funding arrangements. Guidance relating to parent's needs included recommendations for information:

(i) About wards and hospital facilities on admission;
(ii) About the reasons for starvation before operations and on what the child can eat and drink and when;
(iii) About the illness and the operation, preparation for the operation, operating procedures and routines, how to help the child, aftercare, where and how to obtain further information and advice.
(iv) About where parents can wait during the operation, how long the child is likely to be and about what is happening if delays occur;
(v) About what to expect in the recovery room and their role;
(vi) About the likely condition of their child after the operation;
(vii) About the outcome of the operation or procedure at the earliest opportunity by a member of the surgical team and reinforced by the recovery room and ward nurses;
(viii) On how to care for the child after discharge and an emergency number to contact;
(ix) An agreed policy on the information to be given to parents on the ward and a checklist to avoid duplication or conflicting information;
(x) A policy and procedure for interpreting services for families who do not speak;

In 1988, a working party involving the British Paediatric Association, the King's Fund and the National Association of Health Authorities produced guidelines on the care of dying children and their families.These go into considerable detail into the support needs of parents at all stages from diagnosis to bereavement including, for example, the need to:

(i) Ensure that parents are centrally involved and treated with respect as partners in the care;
(ii) Ensure good communication between parents and professionals;
(iii) Ensure that parents have adequate finance;

(iv) Ensure that parents are aware of the range of people (and self-help-groups), both in hospital and in the community, who might help by listening and talking;

(v) Give parents the opportunity to talk to other parents in a similar situation;

(vi) Offer continuity, friendship and sensitive support, responding to individual needs.

Counselling Programmes for Men violence against women in relationships is physical or sexual assault or threat of assault. Violence may occur within ongoing or "separated" relationships, regardless of marital status. Other behaviours such as intimidation, stalking, psychological abuse, sexual abuse, financial exploitation and spiritual abuse should be recognised as part of the continuum of power and control that men use against young and elderly women alike. The following are the some examples in each of these categories:

(i) Physical assault includes grabbing, restraining, slapping, punching, shoving, choking, biting, kicking, shaking, burning with a cigarette, throwing hot liquids, tying up, using weapons (knives, guns, sticks and other objects). Physical abuse also includes the removal of basic necessities (*e.g.*, medications, health care, crutches, food, sleep) and forced alcohol or drug use.

(ii) Psychological abuse includes expressions of excessive jealousy, mistrust, control, threats, verbal abuse and destruction of property. Examples of controlling behaviours include forbidding a woman to go to school, learn English or have a driver's licence. Men who are psychologically abusive may try to limit w hom their partners visit or talk to on the phone, so that the women become isolated from friends and relatives. They may even harass the women at work with repeated phone calls and visits. Examples of threatening behaviours include threatening to use violence against her or her children, to take away the children, to have her deported, to commit suicide if she does not comply with his demands or to have her institutionalised. Non-verbal forms of psychological abuse may include glaring, fist-shaking, physical intimidation and hitting doors or walls.

(iii) Verbal abuse consists of yelling, degrading comments, putdowns, blaming and unfounded accusations about her loyalty or sexual behaviour. It is important to remember that, although a woman who experiences frequent psychological abuse often lives with ongoing fear of her partner, she may never have been the victim of an act that could have brought the man before the courts.

(iv) Sexual abuse and sexual assault are non-consensual, violent acts that compromise the sexual integrity of the victim. These acts include rape, demands for sex in a way that degrades the victim, use of penetrating objects and any form of physical abuse directed at the sexual areas of the body or done during sexual activity. Sexual abuse can also include deliberate infection with HIV or with other sexually transmitted diseases (either refusal to use a condom or failure to reveal the possibility of infection), forcing her to prostitute herself, refusing to take "no" for an answer, initiating sex after violence.

(v) Financial abuse includes denying a woman access to or knowledge of the family's money, preventing her input regarding purchases, forbidding her to have a bank account, denying access to her own money, not paying child support, not allowing her to work or launching legal actions so as to deplete her economic resources.

(vi) Spiritual abuse occurs when a woman's spiritual beliefs are ridiculed or attacked or when she is prevented from attending the religious services of her choice. The man may demand that she attend his religious gatherings or pray in the manner that he dictates. Her children may be raised in a different faith or tradition against her will.

There are a variety of theories explaining men's violence toward their partners. The following are five of the major approaches to understanding men's violence in relationships. Many counsellors and programs are influenced by more than one of the following views:

Psycho-dynamic/Insight Theory

Early theories as to the cause of men's violence against women emphasised psychological problems related to childhood trauma, developmental difficulties or mental illness. Problems include immature personalities, personality disorders, and poor impulse control, fear of intimacy and/or abandonment and psychiatric illnesses.

Some counsellors express concern that attributing men's violence to individual pathology tends to remove responsibility for the behaviour from the perpetrator and place it in the hands of a professional who is to provide treatment.

Dr Anne Ganley, a pioneer in the field, indicates that she did not find a higher proportion of mental illness among men who assault their partners than among men who did not.

However, she did provide a separate counselling group for men, who suffered either from a mental illness requiring medication or had some form of organic brain syndrome. This approach is based on the view that once the organic problem is managed through medication, the man can learn to take responsibility for his abusive behaviour and learn respectful ways of communicating.

Sonkin indicates that for some men, individual therapy can provide an awareness of powerful unconscious emotions, an important first step in taking control of their violence. The danger is that awareness may not necessarily translate into a cessation of violence and the use of power and control at home. If these actions continue to go unchallenged by the criminal justice system, a man's sense of power over her may increase. Other critics of this approach argue that it may not deal with immediate safety issues and ignores the control that the violent behaviour exerts over the victim. Responsible individual counselling focusses on safety concerns first, then explores attitudes that condone violence against women, and finally examines childhood trauma issues.

Ventilation Theory

Although used infrequently as an intervention with assaultive men, the risks associated with this approach warrant mentioning here. Research does not support this theory's main assumption that the ventilation of anger will result in less anger and stress. Tavris reported that venting anger can become addictive to the user.

Straus found that verbal aggression is strongly associated with increases in physical aggression. Ganley expressed concern that when assaultive men release their anger using a punching bag or chopping wood, it can result in reinforcing the behaviour through repetition. In addition, it provides the message that the only way to deal with anger or conflict is through a physical explosion. Ventilating anger suggests that violence is only an anger management problem. This ignores the fact that many men are just as angry in other situations in which they are not violent or controlling.

Family Systems Theory

Usually implemented through couple's therapy, family systems theory (FST) views both victim and perpetrator as participating in maladaptive ways of interacting. Violence serves a function of maintaining distance or reinforcing certain family dynamics already in place. Many feminists voice concern that FST undercuts the seriousness of violence by taking the responsibility for the violence out of the hands of the perpetrator. In addition, FST may ignore the power differences between men and women in our society. Viewing the cause of violence as systemic may indirectly reinforce the view that the woman is responsible for her husband's feelings and actions. Real communication is not possible as long as violence, or the threat of violence, continues.

Cognitive-behavioural and Psycho-educational Theories

These approaches make the violence in the relationship the primary focus of intervention. Because violence is considered to be a learned behaviour, non-violence can be learned as an alternative. The techniques used in a psycho-educational approach include "anger logs" to separate thoughts, feelings and behaviours; time-outs to stop aggressive behaviour; stress management techniques; the identification of dysfunctional thinking that escalates anger; and inter-personal skills training such as communication and assertiveness techniques.

This model has been criticised for taking too narrow a view of men's abusive behaviour and not addressing the function of this behaviour in maintaining power and control over women by individual men and by men as a class.

Pro-feminist Theory

Men's violence is a way to maintain power and control over women. The ways men oppress women through the use of violence include rape, physical aggression and threats. Violence, according to this theory, includes psychological abuse that can undermine the self-esteem of the victim. Two principles have been identified, fundamental to a feminist view of violence against women:

"(i) No woman deserves to be beaten, and
(ii) Men are solely responsible for their actions".

The pro-feminist model supports teaching anger management and communication skills but stresses the need to challenge men's sense of entitlement regarding women and children. Without a challenge to the power imbalance between men and their families, new skills can be misused by men as more sophisticated means to maintain control. From this perspective, work with assaultive men must seek to change social, legal and economic systems that support the oppression of women. Critics of the feminist approach suggest that it ignores individual personality issues that contribute to violence.

In Canada, there is a strong trend toward the use of a psycho-educational model, based on a feminist analysis of men's use of power. Many counsellors are influenced by the work of Alan Jenkins, which assumes that men will change more quickly when they are respected as individuals. In the context of a respectful relationship with a counsellor, a man can be challenged to face the violent and controlling behaviours that, in the long run, are damaging to him as well.

Counselling for assaultive men is just one strategy being promoted in support of the goal of ending violence against women and children. Counselling programs are frequently situated within the community as one part of an overall community intervention approach to ending violence in families. The ground-breaking work of the Duluth Domestic Abuse Intervention Project promotes this type of integrative approach. It stresses the use of a coordinated community response involving the co-operation of the criminal justice system, women's shelters and counselling agencies, assaultive men's intervention programs, and other community members and agencies concerned with ending violence against women in relationships.

Community work may include intervention to stop or prevent child abuse, workshops for students of all ages about non-violent approaches to conflict resolution, and campaigns to educate the public about the frequency and severity of violence against women in relationships.

Alcohol does not cause violence, although it may intensify its nature. A belief in male privilege over women forms the foundation for violent and controlling behaviours. Being drunk or on drugs provides an excuse for many men who say, "I'm only violent when 'I'm high so 'I'm not really a violent person." Although some men are only physically violent when drinking, their use of other forms of power and control generally continues or may escalate when they stop drinking.

A man, who has a problem with alcohol or drug abuse and has been violent, even once, may have two separate problems: one with substance abuse and a second with violence and controlling behaviours. When the immediate threat of violence is removed or reduced through criminal charges, separation, incarceration or other means, it is important that the man begin substance abuse counselling first. If he begins an intervention program for his violence before substance abuse counselling, he is at risk of resorting to drugs or alcohol as an escape from the stress of confronting his abusive behaviour.

A residential treatment centre can provide intensive treatment of his substance abuse and, as a by-product, significantly reduce the risk to his family members. Chemically dependent, assaultive men may enter a substance abuse program assuming that it will also end their violence. In many cases, these men will continue to be abusive even after successfully completing such a program if they do not confront their use of violence and control in relationships.

Research shows that men who drink regularly are more likely to abuse family members. For example, one study shows that fathers who drank to excess were six times as likely to use violence against their own children compared to those who were not heavy drinkers.

This study shows that the rates of wife assault for women living with men who drink regularly is triple the rate of those women whose partners do not drink at all.

Canadian , *National Violence Against Women Survey* indicates that in one half of all violent partnerships, the perpetrator was drinking before an assault. Women whose partners frequently consumed five or more drinks at one time were at six times the risk of violence compared to those whose partners never drank.

The victim may also have a substance abuse problem. Although this may have pre-dated the violent relationship, it may be linked to the man's violence and abuse. He may pressure his partner to drink or use drugs or she may use drugs or alcohol as a means to numb the physical and emotional pain she experiences as a result of ongoing abuse. Women in these situations are especially vulnerable to abusing prescription drugs.

She may receive these from a physician who is treating her for depression or anxiety caused by the violence she is experiencing at home. If she is abusing drugs or alcohol, it may leave her more vulnerable to his violence by compromising her ability to assess danger for herself and her children.

Furthermore, some women prefer to believe that their partner is not violent but only has a drinking problem. It may be hard to face the fact that the man she loves, or at one time did love, is abusive. She will need information and support to help identify other forms of power and control that he may be using when he is not under the influence of alcohol.

Marriage Counselling

Marriage or relationship counselling is based on the assumption that each person feels safe to say what she or he thinks and feels. There are documented cases of couples in marital therapy in which the man threatened or assaulted the woman after a session for saying something that he wanted kept secret, often his violence against her. If either party feels coerced into attending marital therapy, the person should consider individual counselling. When a therapist hears of, or suspects, violence in the relationship, it is important to assess the level of risk by speaking with each partner separately.

If there continues to be a risk of violence and controlling behaviours, the perpetrator should be referred to group or individual counselling focussed on dealing with these issues before relationship counselling continues. Some counsellors place value on keeping the marriage together over the well-being of the individuals in the marriage. The therapist and the husband might imply that, "for the sake of the children," the woman should remain with her husband. Research shows that staying together "for the sake of the children" can be more detrimental than divorce if there is a significant degree of conflict between the parents.

Amato and Keith reviewed a large number of studies examining the effects of divorce on children. Higher rates of problems were evident among children whose parents were in more conflict, whether the couple was still together or divorced, than among children of parents in less conflict.

In some regions of Canada, there are programs for children who are exposed to abuse. Even if a specialized program does not exist, a skilled child therapist can help children cope with feelings related to the abuse and help them realise that they are not to blame. In some provinces, exposure to violence in the home is included in child welfare legislation. In responding to the needs of a family in which woman abuse has occurred, it is important to keep in mind the needs of the children for safety and security.

When professionals suspect child abuse, they have a legal duty to report to child protection authorities. The father's access may have to be restricted or supervised in situations where children have witnessed violence or been the victims of abuse.

Professionals should be aware that children may need support and/or counselling after these visits. The woman may need extensive support, both legal and emotional, to resist allowing the father contact with the children when it is not in their best interest.

Several provinces now have a professional association of counsellors who work with assaultive men. These associations also have, in many cases, formal standards of practice. To help you identify some basic issues, obtain a copy of the standards from the association in your province or territory. These associations often maintain lists of member counsellors of programs who subscribe to the standards of practice.

Men who are violent and abusive in their relationships have the same variety of problems that non-violent men do. Some men will benefit from individual therapy as well as group therapy.

Before embarking on counselling for their assaultive behaviour, some men will require substance abuse counselling first. During group counselling, traumatic childhood issues may arise and the men may require individual counselling as well. Men who suffer from a mental illness will require psychiatric assessment and treatment for the mental illness, in addition to group counselling for violence. When the abusive and controlling behaviour has stopped and the woman feels safe, the two may wish to participate in relationship counselling.

Men who are veterans or immigrants from war-torn countries may need additional help with issues related to torture or other experiences that may have produced post-traumatic stress disorder. Responsible programs screen out men who are not likely to benefit. Criteria for exclusion may include the following: Active and untreated substance abuse problems, severe mental illness, high lethality, extreme denial, and brain injury. Entering a group therapy program can increase risk in some cases, as some men meet any challenge with violence or *intimidation.*

Counselling programs should not be a substitute for jail. Men who have spent some time in jail for assaulting their partner often report that the experience of going to jail helped them stop and think twice about using violence again. Although anger management skills are taught in most counselling programs, they are not the same. Anger management can be described as focussing on "three main areas:

(i) stress management and relaxation training,
(ii) identification of emotions and cognitive restructuring, and
(iii) interpersonal skills development".

Anger management can help a man to stop his violence and recognise that he can control his anger and be responsible for his behaviour. However, counselling that focusses mainly on anger management misses the point that violence may only be resorted to by a man when other techniques to maintain control over his partner have not been effective. Furthermore, many men feel just as angry with others in their lives but do not "lose control" and become violent. It is important for counselling programs to assist men in confronting the attitudes about women that make her feelings, needs and ideas less important than his.

Some ethnic communities run their own programs that address culturally specific conditions contributing to violence and allow men to express themselves in their own language. These programs should be accessed whenever possible. Programs for specific ethnic communities will address the same core issues as programs for the dominant culture, but will present these in culturally sensitive ways.

When men of visible and ethnic minorities enter mainstream programs for assaultive men, it is important that counsellors are aware of the impact that immigration, extended family issues and differing beliefs, attitudes and values have upon these clients.

The man's counsellor or another staff person from his program should be in touch with the partner of an abusive man. Initially, the practitioner will want to talk to her about the relationship and the history and nature of the violence and abuse.

At this time, she should be given information about formulating a safety plan, if she does not already have one. She should be referred to counselling, support, and legal services for herself and her children. Periodically, she should be contacted to ascertain whether there has been any recurrence of violence or threats.

Without this type of follow-up, there is no mechanism by which to gauge the effectiveness of the program. Every woman should know that she has a right to her privacy and may, at any time, refuse to respond to requests of information by the program.

If she chooses, the woman may be apprised of her partner's attendance, the length and content of the program, but not the details of the discussions that take place during her partner's counselling. Some communities will not have programs for assaultive men but will have counsellors who provide standard counselling services only to individuals. The woman has the right to expect the above basic in formation from any counsellor.

Counselling is not an "instant fix." However, his use of physical violence and threats should stop immediately. If not, the degree of his commitment to change may be questionable.

A woman should anticipate that he will begin to remove himself from the home or take "time-outs" when he starts to get angry, and that he will stop other abusive, intimidating and controlling behaviours. In time, he should be able to listen to her concerns and demonstrate respect for her as an individual with needs and wants which are different from his own.

Women should be cautioned that some men may stop violent or threatening behaviours that could have legal consequences but escalate other controlling or manipulative tactics to maintain a position of domination in the relationship. A man's attending counselling is not a guarantee that he will stop his use of violence and controlling behaviours. Underneath a thin veneer of normalcy, women who have been victims of violence often feel isolated, confused and powerless, and suffer from low self-esteem.

Supportive counselling by a woman-centred agency or counsellor experienced in working with assaulted women can help the victim understand that the violence is not her fault. It can help her decide how she can take steps to protect herself and her children and what legal means are available to her.

Because a man has completed a counselling program, it does not mean that she "owes" him reconciliation. Pressures to reunite, in the form of promises to change, gifts and tears, threats over child custody or support, and demands to accept his apology, are examples of his continued abuse and attempts to exert control over her life.

Even though there are groups for assaultive men in every major Canadian city and in many rural areas, not all men can or will change their violent and abusive behaviour. A woman may want the counsellor to tell her if her partner is safe to live with again, yet she is really the best judge of her own safety. Some men make good use of a group program and can become respectful and caring partners. Others may appear to learn and participate in the group, but maintain a domineering approach to their partner and children in the home.

Even if the counselling appears to have helped the man, it is still important to provide the woman with support and information about a safety plan, legal means and where to go for counselling for herself and her children. When women are violent toward their partners, it is often self-defence. In some cases, the woman is the one to initiate and sustain the violence. Although there is an ongoing debate over the extent to which women use violence in relationships, many more women are seriously harmed and killed by their spouse than are men.

In British Columbia, the Policy on Violence against Women in Relationships is intended to cover "vulnerable males" as well as the assault of women. Men commonly minimise the frequency and severity of violence and abuse. Women may do so as well, unable to acknowledge the frequency and severity of the abuse they live with, or in response to his demands to keep it a secret.

It is important to realise that physical violence is just one form of power and control and that financial abuse, psychological abuse, intimidation, isolation, sexual pressure and sexual assault can have an equally damaging impact on the victim. For these reasons, even a man who has truly used physical violence for the first time should receive counselling that focusses on his use of power and control in his relationship.

Individual Psychotherapy

Individual psychotherapy can help an assaultive man explore issues from his past, examine attitudes that contribute to his domination of women, and learn skills to establish healthy relationships. However, group therapy with other men who share the same problems can reduce isolation, denial and minimisation and provide a positive experience of real peer support. Men, who are hostile and resistant to the idea of going to a group for "wife-beaters" will often open up more quickly and begin to take responsibility for their actions when they interact with a group of men who have similar problems.

By attending group counselling, men can learn different ways of relating to other men, including honestly discussing feelings and issues and showing respect when discussing women, rather than stereo-typing them. In communities where appropriate group therapy for assaultive men is not available, individual therapy with a professional with the appropriate knowledge and skill is the next best alternative. The majority of programs run from three to six months. Just because a man has completed a program of any length is no guarantee that he is safe and respectful in his relationships with women.

For this reason, several programs have a policy of expelling men who either do not participate or actively maintain a closed and hostile attitude. No number of sessions will help change a man, who continues to blame his partner and/or the criminal justice system for his behaviour or who refuses to make a commitment to change. When a man realises that improving his ways of relating to everyone in his life is a life-long process, he is on his way.

7

Organisation of Guidance Services

Introduction

The organisation of guidance services is gradually acquiring importance in our country. Sporadic efforts in the past on individual basis are being replaced by formalised guidance services. Educationists are now convinced that organised guidance services should be available in all higher secondary schools to prepare adolescents to develop their abilities to the maximum in a democratic society. Needless to mention that in the last two decades several revolutionary changes have taken place in our society. The enormous growth in our population, use of technology in all sectors — medicine, business, industry and increased job opportunities for skilled and semi-skilled professions — all these have necessitated the introduction of guidance services.

The reader may now ask a simple question: What are the advantages of organized guidance services? Some of the advantages are enumerated below.

Advantages of Organised Guidance Programmme

(a) ***Coordination.*** It makes possible coordinating work of staff members, guidance personnel and social worker so that instead of divergent, unrelated types of activities, the work of each person will relate to that of others in an integrated pattern.

(b) ***Avoidance of duplication.*** The unnecessary duplication of effort can be easily avoided. An organised programme makes it possible to plan for the most pressing needs. It increases the efficiency of the services.

(c) ***Maximum utilisation of services:*** Organisation facilitates the use of skills, training and interest of individual staff members and utilises their services to the maximum.

(d) ***Economy of time and effort:*** A third advantage of organisation is the economy of time and effort by the principal as well as the staff members involved.

(e) ***Spirit of cooperative participation:*** Finally, an organised approach to guidance should result in increased cooperation among the staff. A member is able to know the responsibilities of others as well as his own and can participate as a team member in promotion of guidance services.

Characteristics of a Good Guidance Programme

Guidance programme should be organised on certain principles if it is really meant to provide efficient services to the pupils. Following are some of the characteristics of a good guidance programme.

(i) A modern guidance programme is keyed to the purposes of education. A good programme should be aimed to achieve the purposes of education.

(ii) A good guidance programme assists children to resolve conflicts arising from modern society. Many conditions which affect adolescents are given below:

(a) Changes in the role of home and family.

(b) Shifts from rural to urban modes of living.

(c) Conflicts in social values.

(d) Rapid scientific development and the lag in adaptive social process

(e) Developmental changes in physical, emotional, social and intellectual abilities.

(iii) A good guidance programme is an integral part of education. Both cannot be separated.

(iv) It helps the school staff to understand better the characteristics of all adolescents and the problems which emerge during adolescence.

(v) It supplies information which may be useful in planning experiences for all.

(vi) It uses guidance data in promotional policy, and practice, in grouping within the classroom and in special placement of individuals.

(vii) It emphasizes and applies principles of learning.

(viii) It improves classroom relationship and emotional climate through emphasis upon democratic procedures.

(ix) It provides for adolescents with special needs.

(x) It is a collective responsibility of many staff members and the administrator.

(xi) It stimulates the professional growth of all personnel.

(xii) It improves ways of working with parents and community.

(xiii) It utilises community service resources which can contribute to the welfare of adolescents.

(xiv) It focusses attention upon the importance of evaluation, and uses appropriate techniques of evaluating the educational programme of the school.

Functions of a Secondary School Guidance Programme

The functions of guidance programme in a secondary school are as follows:

(i) To assist the individual student to achieve an increasing degree of maturity in working toward the solution of his varied personal adjustment problems. A majority of students in a higher secondary and an intermediate college are between the ages of twelve and eighteen years of age who face a number of problems in home, school and society due to developmental changes. The guidance programme should assist adolescents to understand their problems and to recognise resources which may be helpful in solving them. The guidance programme should be organised in such a way that the first goal is achieved by means of the following ways:

(a) Helping the individual to develop a better understanding of himself.
(b) Helping the individual and understanding of his opportunities.
(c) Helping the individual to set up realistic goals to develop sound plans to achieve them.
(d) Helping the individual to acquire the ability to handle problems of human relationship
(e) Helping the individual to bridge the gaps between different goals 2. To assist the school staff in securing, interpreting, and using information concerning the characteristics, needs and opportunities of students.

The collection of useful data about individuals and groups of students requires the cooperation of the entire school staff. A guidance worker needs the help of teachers in gathering information from guidance personnel.

(a) Material useful in developing a curriculum that meets the needs.
(b) Information useful to modify classroom procedures which includes information on the following:
(i) Readings for learning. (ii) Achievement in various subjects. (iii) Special interests of students. (iv) Health and personality problems. (v) Personal goals and objectives. (vi) Personal problems of students in schools. (vii) Problems of drop-outs and those who have left the school. 3. To assist the school and its staff in understanding aind working closely with the community they serve.

There must be close cooperation between the school and the community. A sound relationship can be established with the following activities:

(a) encouraging parent participation.
(b) visiting home.
(c) developing contacts with employers and representatives of the community.
(d) working closely with other community organizations.

(i) *Counselling.* The school should assist the individual to understand his problems and help him in the planning of possible solutions to his problems.

(ii) *Placement.* Helping students to find out jobs according to their interests, aptitudes and mental abilities.

(iii) *Follow-up.* Maintaining contacts with all school leavers and checking individual achievement for the purpose of evaluating and improving guidance programme. Research should be conducted on different aspects of guidance services.

Some Basic Principles of Guidance Services

(i) Guidance services are an integral part of the total education programme.

(ii) A sound guidance programme evolves out of cooperative planning and effort of the entire school staff. It grows in relationship to the needs of the school, community and individual characteristics.

(iii) The principal is the key figure who provides leadership.

(iv) The responsibility may be delegated to a senior member in big schools.

(v) It provides services to all students.

(vi) Duties should be assigned to competent members.

(vii) In-service training of the staff is essential.

(viii) Counsellors and other guidance personnel should be assigned duties that will make use of their abilities. Routine clerical work should not be given to them.

(ix) The effectiveness of competent counsellors can be materially increased through the provision of time, materials and personnel necessary for the maintenance of records.

(x) The guidance programme of a school can be greatly strengthened if it can call on the community for a number of services.

Problems in Organising Guidance Services

(i) Physical facilities for the guidance programme: The first problem which guidance services face in the higher secondary schools where they exist in this country are that they are housed very poorly. There is no separate accommodation provided for these services.

(ii) Counsellor's load of work. The load of counsellor's work is so much that he cannot do justice to his job. Most of his time is wasted in clerical work.

(iii) Methods of assigning students to counsellors. Students are assigned to counsellors at random.

(iv) Organisation of counselling staff. The counselling staff is not well organised and well qualified to meet the needs of students.

Pattern of Organisation

No single pattern or structure of organising guidance can suit the needs of all schools — large and small, rural and urban, girls and boys. The organisational pattern should be planned in accordance with the needs of the schools and the facilities available in terms of building, finance and staff.

Two tentative patterns are given here — one, for a typical higher secondary school and the other for organising guidance services at the state level. The reader should keep in his mind that they do not represent ideal plans. Rather they are practical adaptations of the ideal to local conditions. Modifications according to local conditions can be made in the plans.

The pattern of organising guidance services for a higher secondary school can be as follows:

(i) ***Principal:*** The principal is the overall incharge of the administration and organization of guidance services in his school. He should provide space, finance and direction to the organisation. The principal may delegate his responsibilities to one of the senior members of the staff interested in guidance services.

(ii) ***Teacher:*** A member of faculty may be given the responsibilities of administering the programme. All teachers should be encouraged to participate in the guidance programme.

(iii) ***Counsellor:*** A qualified and competent counsellor should be appointed.

(iv) *Committee.* A committee should be formed to look after the total organization and functioning of the programme.

Organisation at the State Level

(a) Director of Education.
(b) Deputy Director of Guidance Services.
(c) District Guidance Officer.

(a) ***Director of Education:*** The director of education is the incharge of education in the state from pre-primary to university level. There are some big states where there are separate directors for primary, secondary and university education. The Director of Education should be the overall incharge of guidance services in the state.

(b) ***Deputy director, guidance services:*** In a big state more than one deputy directors may be appointed as incharge of guidance services. The deputy director should coordinate the guidance services provided in the district under his charge.

(c) ***District guidance centre:*** A guidance centre should be opened at the district headquarter in every district. The staff should consist of a psychologist, counsellor and a guidance officer incharge of the centre. The centre should coordinate the services of higher secondary schools in the district and should also provide guidance to the guidance workers.

(d) ***School guidance workers:*** Every higher secondary school must have a competent and qualified guidance worker. The number of guidance workers may be raised keeping in view the strength of the school. A school having strength upto 1000 (one thousand) should appoint at least one guidance worker who should be assisted by a senior staff member. Separate accommodation should be provided for guidance services.

(e) ***School guidance committee:*** A committee consisting of the principal, teachers, community leaders and parents should be appointed in every higher secondary school to advise the guidance worker to facilitate his work. Parents and community leaders can play an important role in appraising the committee of the general problems and needs of the adolescents. The guidance committee should meet to review the cases of problem children.

8

Evaluation of Guidance

Introduction

Evaluation is the process of finding the value of something. It consists of making systematic judgments of the relative effectiveness with which goals are attained in relation to specified standards. It is an important aspect of guidance programme to evaluate its effectiveness because it throws light on the strengths and weaknesses of the programme and consequently helps in improving the programmes in the light of the data.

Another important reason to evaluate the guidance services is that the community is interested to know whether guidance services have produced some specific desirable benefits — demonstrable behavioural change in students. Such evidence can be secured only through evaluation of, and research on, guidance programme.

Evaluation of guidance programme is mandatory if the effectiveness of its services is to be known and if its services are to be improved. Therefore, systematic evaluation of guidance programme enables the school personnel to judge how well they are. doing and provides bases for deciding the nature of improvement in curriculum and classroom instructional methodology. If the systematic evaluation is not conducted, there is every possibility that the decisions that are made will often be shaped by prejudice, by traditions or by rationalisation. Parents need to be informed of the present status of a programme if they are to participate intelligently in it and also assist in defining its directions and objectives. Therefore, it is very essential to evaluate periodically the effectiveness and efficiency of guidance programme.

In India, no evaluation at state or national level has so far been conducted to see the effectiveness of guidance services which are provided to students in schools and colleges. It is urgently needed to conduct a survey of existing guidance services to see their weaknesses and strengths so that in future remedial measures may be taken to improve them.

Basic Steps in Evaluation of Guidance Programme

Researchers in the field of guidance during the last two decades in the West have developed-various approaches to evaluate the guidance services provided in schools. As regards our country, guidance services have not made much progress in the last twenty years. They are at the initial stage. A time may come when we would need the evaluation of guidance in future. There are certain basic elements which are inherent in any comprehensive evaluative process. These are as follows:

a. ***Specification of objectives:*** The first and foremost step is to clarify the objectives of the programme in observable behavioural terms. The anticipated outcomes of whatever is being done must be formulated in such a manner that they can be observed and verified objectively, with the help of some objective criteria.
b. ***Methods:*** Decide in advance the methods and techiniques that are to be used to attain the objectives.
c. ***Examine data:*** Examine the available data about students to determine if they include tests and measurements and. other relevant information about students.
d. ***Procedure:*** A procedure must be developed to collect evidence as to whether the activities of methods will result in the attainment of objectives.
e. ***Cooperation:*** Consider the extent of cooperation with employers and school personnel, because without the active cooperation of school personnel, no systematic research may be conducted.

f. ***Judgement:*** The last step is to make judgments about the attainment of objectives of guidance and suggest remedial steps to improve upon the existing conditions.

Methods of Evaluation

There are three methods which are generally used to evaluate guidance programmes. They are briefly described as follows:

A. Survey Method

Survey method is the most frequently used appraisal method in the school setting to evaluate the effectiveness of guidance services. This method usually focusses upon the intent and presence of certain services, the number of staff personnel, their qualifications, and use of time, physical facilities and other external factors.

Though, survey method involves both objective and subjective judgments, it gives little evidence as to whether student behaviour is significantly affected by services.

The following steps are followed in survey method:

1. Selection of predetermined criteria for inventory.
2. Collection of evidence of the services being offered.
3. Making judgments regarding the degree to which these services are provided with reference to the predetermined criteria.

In survey method, the following techniques can be used to collect data to evaluate the guidance services:

(a) ***Simple observation:*** The -effects of educational and vocational guidance programme can be surveyed by using observational technique of evaluation. The effectiveness may be judged to some extent by a reduction in the problems of students, reduction in reports of indiscipline to the principal, attendance improvement, reaction of parents to guidance programme as shown by the attendance in parent-teachers' association meetings.

(b) ***Check list, questionnaire or rating sheet:*** Check list, questionnaire and rating sheet can be prepared to evaluate the guidance services provided in different schools and industrial undertakings. A check list can provide information from teachers, parents, managers, and community agencies on different aspects of guidance services.

B. Experimental Method

Experimental method is the most systematic approach to conduct research study in any area of knowledge. It is carefully planned to study one or more groups of individuals in terms of one or more variables. Generally, the following steps are followed in an experimental study:

(a) Determination of objectives and methods of attaining these objectives.
(b) The development of ways to measure the attainment of these objectives.
(c) Selection of control and experimental groups.
(d) The process of carrying out necessary steps for the attainment of objectives.
(e) Measurement of the outcome of experimentation.

C. Case Study Method

The case study method is designed to assess the changes that take place in an individual as a result of introducing a variable such as counselling. Goals appropriate to the individual are formulated. Counselling takes place. Data are collected on progress towards the goal. These steps are followed, reviewed and assessment of changes in the individual that are attributable to the procedure employed is reported. This method has certain limitations. For exmaple, it depends on subjective evaluation and is also time-consuming.

Limitations of Evaluative Methods

All evaluative methods to assess the outcome of guidance programmes have certain limitations.

i. There is lack of clear acceptable objectives of guidance programmes.
ii. Methods of evaluating guidance services fail to relate students objectives to all institutional educational objectives.

iii. Use of immediate and easily available criteria and failure to validate such criteria against long-term goals.
iv. Individual differences are ignored.
v. All methods make excessive use of subjective reactions.
vi. All methods give little attention to satisfactory experimental designs.

The Criteria for Successful Guidance Programme

a. ***Reduction in scholastic failure:*** Guidance services may be effective if they enable the students to select courses of study commensurate with their abilities and consequently aid in reducing the scholastic failure in schools. They should enable the students to cope with their academic difficulties.
b. ***Reduction in discipline problems:*** A successful programme is expected to reduce the problems of students indiscipline in schools by providing them opportunities for the resolution of tensions and conflicts etc.
c. ***Greater utilisation of the counselling services***: A programme may be called successful if the people use the facilities' provided and are benefited by them.
d. ***Reduction in programme changes:*** Systematically planned guidance services should enable the students to have a sound plan for educational and vocational career.

   The students should be made less prone to whimsical and frequent changes in their plans.
e. ***Choice of suitable vocational goals:*** Guidance services should make a student aware of vocational opportunities and should enable him to make vocational choice consistent with his ability and interest. Guidance should eliminate both wastage of talent and choice of unrealistic goals.

Steps to Secure Change in Guidance Services

Researchers have mentioned some steps which if properly followed will help in bringing changes in the presently available guidance services.

a. ***Establish commitment to change:*** The counsellor, administrator and the teachers should make a determined effort to bring changes for the improvement of guidance programme. No change can be secured by half-hearted efforts.

b. ***Determine the needs:*** Before starting to secure change, it is usually better to list the most pressing needs of change. For this purpose, a thorough and careful appraisal of the total programme should be conducted. The changes should be planned on the basis of money, time and personnel available.
c. ***Study the school situation:*** The guidance workers should use their diagnostic skills to determine which individuals are most complacent with regard to present practices.
d. ***Clarify the present status:*** Guidance personnel who wish to introduce change must perform three fuctions: (a) clarify present status (self-concept by evaluation), (b) describe the desired programme, and (c) point out discrepancies and introduce the aspect of needed innovation.
e. ***Gain administrative support:*** If some change is designed then it is necessary to gain the administrative support because without administrative support far-reaching improvements are unlikely to be made or if instituted, they will have no lasting or pervasive effect.
f. ***Involve the staff:*** To bring changes, the active participation of the staff is very essential. When teachers are unable to identify with modifications and accept responsibility to make use of them, there is little likelihood that improvement will last.
g. Acquaint the community with the reasons and necessity of change. Every community has certain expectations with respect to school programmes. So if some changes are to be affected the community should be aware of the necessity and urgency of the change. The cooperation of various agencies working in the community should be sought to bring changes in the programme of the school.

An Evaluation Model for Guidance

Traditionally, decisions that affect guidance programme development and upgrading have not been based on systematic evaluation. Instead, decision-makers mostly have relied on insight, trial and error and other pseudo-scientific methods which have failed to evaluate objectively the guidance programme.

Edward Paul Dworkin and Garry R. Walz evolved recently an evaluation model for guidance which may be used to evaluate systematically guidance programmes. Their model is meant to evaluate career guidance services rather than for guidance broadly defined. The model for evaluation in guidance is briefly as follows.

Their model has the following features:

i. The model places guidance within the context of the nature of man, the nature of society and the nature of educative process.
ii. It treats guidance as a result as well as focussing on each of its component parts and the inter-relation of its parts to one another and the whole.
iii. It is relevant to important goals or outcomes.
iv. It provides necessary information so that decisions can be made at appropriate times concerning any aspect of programme development.
v. It considers long-term as well as short-term evaluation.

Conceptual Framework

The guidance evaluation model has been based on the following assumptions:

***Assumption 1*:** Man engages in meaningful goal-directed activity. Individuals need more assistance with their career development and adjustment in home work.

Assumption 2: Society has a need to maintain itself and develop and this need can only be achieved if individuals engage in meaningful behaviour that both maintains and develops the society in which they live. Society must provide the necessary training for career development and adjustment to the individuals.

Assumption 3: Career development and adjustment is a continuous life-long process.

Assumption 4: An important goal of the educative process is to assist persons with their career development and adjustment so that they can satisfy their own unique needs and the needs of society.

Assumption 5: All educational endeavours are processes; they are not justified in themselves but only as they yield progress toward desired goals. The structural components of schools should function in an integrative manner to facilitate attainment of goals.

Assumption 6: The schools and other educative agencies should make continual adjustments in their structural make-up to accommodate the ever-changing needs of society. Failure to this may lead to irrelevancy and rebellion.

Assumption 7: The focus of the educative process is on the individual. If schools are to act as behavioural change agents, it is imperative that the persons to be changed are understood from many points of view. The needs of the individual should be identified at different points of time in the developmental continuum in order to develop learning experiences that will integrate these needs into the structural make-up of schools.

Assumption 8: It is essential that school and other educative agencies should work together toward the attainment of goals.

Expanding the Conceptual Work

The conceptual framework described above suggestions that guidance can serve a very central and functional role in the educative process. The following operations should be performed to translate the conceptual framework into practical terms:

i. Identify the need of the population with which your work.
ii. Identify and describe the relevant characteristics and needs of the coummunity as well as the basic characteristics and needs of the country as a whole.
iii. Develop the objectives of career guidance programmes on the bases of individual and environmental in-puts. Objectives of the programme should be clearly specified in behavioural terms so that they can be assessed and ranked in terms of priority.
iv. The next step is to select the most feasible setting in which to implement the established objectives in whole or in part. It is

important to identify and deal with constraints found in the selected settings with a view to make desirable changes.

v. A variety of methods for accomplishing the specified objectives must then be identified and developed. Innovative methods such as computer-based career guidance system should be used.

vi. The degree to which each specified objective has been accomplished must be ascertained. This information can then serve as feedback to the planning and decision-making process that allows redesign and continuous improvement of the overall programme on a rational basis.

Career Guidance Evaluation Model

The six steps described above are cumulative in nature and should be performed in sequential order. They comprise the basic elements of a systems approach in the development of career guidance programmes. The following are the various parts of the system which should be periodically evaluated to modify the programme:

a. ***Individual Input Evaluation:*** The purposes of individual input evaluation are to identify the career needs of those individuals we wish to assist and to delineate problems underlying these needs. Career needs of young children and adults should be identified. There is great need to identify the needs of women and retired persons and other disadvantaged groups in our society, because women have recently started entering all types of professions. And retired persons also seek some goal-directed activity to utilise their time in a purposeful way.

b. ***Environmental Input Evaluation:*** Environmental input evaluation allows the researcher to describe the environment, the unmet needs of the environment and problems underlying these needs. This means to describe the manpower needs and other related career aspects of the environment and describing the means by which the environment is meeting the career needs of citizens; and delineating problems associated with these. Decisions served by environmental input evaluation include the focussing of priority manpower needs of the community and country and strategies for utilising existing community resources. Information generated from individual and environmental input evaluation will help build a stable foundation on which to develop objectives for career guidance programmes.

c. ***Objective Evaluation:*** The success of career guidance programme largely depends on the degree to which meaningful objectives have been specified. The formulation of objectives should be based on information generated from the two previous evaluation activities. The objectives should meet the following criteria:

(i) They should evolve from a sound conceptual framework.
(ii) They should derive from an integrating basic philosophy.
(iii) They should be stated in terms of behavioural changes.
(iv) They should be realistically achievable within a specified time period.
(v) They should be amenable to evaluation.
(vi) They should incorporate recognition of career needs.
(vii) Thev should be capable of being translated into practice.
(viii) They should be stated in sequence.
(ix) They should be independent.
(x) They should be flexible.

d. ***Setting Evaluation:*** Setting evaluation allows us to identify the most appropriate setting in which to implement career guidance objectives as a whole or in part, and to identify strategies for dealing with constraints associated with selected setting. It is desirable to consider a variety of potential settings in which to implement career guidance objectives. The selection of appropriate setting should be based on careful analyses of potential strengths and weaknesses of a number of potential settings. Potential setting should be assessed in terms of time, money, resources, potential procedural barriers etc.

e. ***Process Evaluation:*** Process evaluation is an important step to identify and develop appropriate methods for accomplishing the career guidance objectives and to identify the potential sources of failure in the programme. Developing and selecting methods include surveying the literature, consulting with authorities, visiting innovative career guidance programmes and using individual creativity.

f. **Pro*duct Evaluation:*** Product evaluation provides information for making decisions to continue, modify, refocus or terminate as activity found in previous evaluation stages.

9

Occupational Information and Job Satisfaction

Introduction

Tremendous explosion of knowledge in science and technology in the modern days has enriched the store house of information. The scientific and technological advancements have brought in many changes in social and economic structure of our country. Among the many challenges faced by our youths today is the choice of a right career. The occupational information, one of the important components of guidance programme is basic to career planning and adjustment. This unit provides you an overview of meaning, need and sources of occupational information, methods of collection, classification and filing of occupational information, and techniques of dissemination of occupational information. It also familiarizes you with factors affecting jobsatisfation, job analysis, job specifications and job profile.

Objectives

After going through this unit you will be able to:

- Explain the need and importance of occupational information in the present day;
- List different sources of occupational information, i.e., primary secondary, international, national and local;

- List different methods of collection of occupational information
- Describe various techniques of dissemination of occupational information;
- Identify various factors of job satisfaction;
- Point out the relationship between job analysis, job specifications and job profile.

Concept and Needs of Occupational Information

Concept: Occupational information is information about the world of work'. Occupational information covers pertinent and reliable information relating to various occupations e.g., job contents, training and preparation for the occupation, entry in to occupation, working conditions, salaries, emoluments, employment outlooks and prospects etc.

***Need and Importance*:** Occupational information service is one of the important guidance services. The need and importance of occupational information is as follows.

Career Planning: Due to vastness of educational and occupational opportunities available today the student needs accurate reliable and useful information. Occupational information is one of the essential aspects of career planning.

Career Development: Occupational information is also essential for career development of students. The individual's appropriate skills, attitudes, interests, abilities, values and self concept depend upon accurate information about specific jobs.

Vocational thinking: In the early stage i.e elementary stage, occupational information helps to widen the vocational thinking. This helps them to explore the vocational world.

Changing Perceptions: Occupational information helps to check the pre conceived distorted notion of individual regarding some job.

Placement: As the student gets reliable and accurate information about the job, through occupational information it helps in placement. The student gets information about personality traits required for a particular job, which helps in getting the job. Apart from this, occupational information has important role inpreparation of selection tests for jobs, upgradation of skills of employed manpower and international comparison of occupational data.

Collection, Filing and Classification of Occupational Information

Sources of Occupational Information: There is array of sources for bringing occupational information materials in different forms for use by teachers, counselors and students. These sources can be classified on the basis of nature and scope of information.

On the basis of nature of the source of occupational information, it is classified as Primary and Secondary source of information.

On the basis of the scope of information it is classified as International, National and Local.

Primary and Secondary Sources: The primary source is the original or direct source from here we get the relevant occupational information. The information collected from the employer, employee/worker, and government bodies/agencies are example of primary sources.

The secondary sources of information are those which use information collected or published by the original sources.

These are also called indirect sources. International, National, Local Sources: Many international, national and state/local level organisations/agencies bring out publications related to occupations. Some of the International, national and state/local level sources are given below:

Types of Occupational Information Materials: The materials prepared by different agencies, institutions for occupational information broadly classified in to three types, i.e., print material, audiovisual materials and electronic materials:

Print Materials	*Audio/Visual*	*Electronic*
Occupational Monographs Employment News News-Paper and Magazines Recruitment Literatures Occupa?	Career films Career photographs Posters and charts Audio	Radio Television Computers

Before using any material, you need to evaluate the accuracy, relevance, format and usefulness of the information.

Methods of Collection of Occupational Information: How can you collect occupational information? The occupational information can be collected through various methods i.e., follow up surveys, community occupational survey, community educational survey and want ad survey.

Follow up Survey: The follow up survey can be conducted to find out career adjustments of school leavers. These provide information about educational and employment opportunities in the community. The occupational facts provided by the survey help the school students to plan their career realistically.

***Community Occupational Survey*:** The community educational survey is an enumeration and description of jobs in a geographically defined area. The survey provides an overview of occupational information about community specific occupations, man power trends and requirements. If you want to conduct a community occupational survey, you have to visit with your colleagues to a near by office/agency/industry and obtain relevant information on name and address of the organisation, existing occupations, man power requirements i.e. job openings, eligibility, requirements and salary. Community Educational Survey:

A community educational survey is conducted to collect detailed information about educational institutions in a particular geographical area. This survey covers all types of educational institutions such as schools, colleges (medical, engineering, vocational), distance education centers etc. Relevant information collected on courses offered, number of seats, procedure of admission, fees, hostel, scholarship etc will give insight.

The prospectus, information bulletin of different institutions can be studied and analysed to compare educational facilities.

Want –Ad Survey: This is the simplest and least expensive survey. It is a periodic (weekly, monthly, quarterly) tabulation of the job openings as advertised in newspapers. Here two types of advertisements, i.e., help want ads and situation vacant ad appearing in local newspapers or neighbuoring metropolitan newspapers are used. While the first type advertisement provides information regarding job openings the second type of ads provide data of supply of workers for possible job openings. The tabulation of data in this survey may be done according to broad group of classification (NCO), based on interst, curricular streams etc. Want ad surveys are of great value to metropolitan and small cities.

Classification of Occupational Information: Collection of a lot of occupational information necessitates storing it in a systematic manner so that can be used by others with out difficulty whenever required. For a meaningful storage of occupational information we have to know different ways of classifying information. Occupational information can be classified in a number of ways such as by occupation, industry, socio-economic status, interests, and educational levels etc. All these classification schemes have their own merits and limitations. Some of the classification schemes are discussed below.

Classification by Occupation: *National Classification of Occupation (NCO-2004)* — As per the NCO-2004 occupations have been classified into the following nine divisions and skill levels.

Division Title Skill Level

(i) Legislatures, Senior Officials and Managers;
(ii) Professionals,
(iii) Technicians and Associate professionals,
(iv) Clerks,
(v) Service workers and shop, market sales workers,
(vi) Skilled agricultural and fishery workers,
(vii) Craft and related trade workers,
(viii) Plant and machine operators and assemblers,
(ix) Elementary Occupations

NCO-2004 groups together 2945 occupations, each occupations has been assigned a six digit code, a distinct title and a definition. The occupations have been first assigned to ten occupational divisions (identified by the initial digit in the code number) that are comprised of thirty sub-divisions (identified by first two digit of the code number).The subdivisions have 116 groups (identified by first three digit of the code number).

Classification by Industry

National Industrial Classification-2004*(NIC-2004)*: The Central Statistical Organisation (CSO) has developed the NIC-2004 in India. It has 17 sections, 62 Divisions, 161 groups, 310 classes and 1191 subclasses. The 17 sections are listed by one letter alpha code from A to Q as below.

(A) Agriculture, hunting and forestry,
(B) Fishing,
(C) Mining and quarrying,
(D) Manufacturing,
(E) Electricity, gas and water supply,
(F) Construction,
(G) Wholesale and retail trade; repair of motor vehicles, motor cycles and personal and household goods.
(H) Hotels and restaurants,
(I) Transport, storage and communication,
(J) Financial intermediation,
(K) Real estate, renting and business activities,
(L) Public administration and defence; compulsory social security,
(M) Education,
(N) Health and social work,
(O) Other community, social and personal service activities,
(P) Activities of private households as employers and undifferentiated production activities of households.
(Q) Extraterritorial organisations and bodies.

The NIC-2004 adopts a five digit classification where the first two digits indicate Division, the first three digits represent Group, and four digits indicate Class. The sub-classes (if exists) are indicated by all the five numbers. The NIC-2004 has been used in the country for population census, industrial survey etc.

Classification Based on Interest

In this classification scheme, occupations are categorised according to interest areas. Comprehensive Interest Schedule by Vohra (1993) lists eight interest areas i.e., influential, venturous, artistic, scientific, analytical, social, nature and clerical. The type of occupation-related to interests are administrative and enterprising (Influential), Defence and Sports (venturous), Creative and performing (Artistic), Medical and technical (Scientific), Expressive and computational (analytical), Humanitarian and education (social).

Filing of Occupational Information: In school situation educational/occupational information may be available in both bound and unbound form. The unbound materials may include leaflets, folders, newspaper clippings, notice etc. Similarly the bound materials include proseptus, hand book, information brochures etc. Some popular filing plans for unbound information materials are alphabetic Plan, Classification based upon educational level, based on academic subjects or curricular stream and geographical files etc.

Alphabetic Plan: In this system, occupational information is classified according to the first alphabet of each occupation. Here, ccupational headings to be used are collected from occupational or industrial classification. Classification based upon Educational Level: Various Levels of education i.e. elementary school, secondary school, higher secondary school, post school diploma certificate, graduation, post graduation and M.Phil/Doctorate. Classification based on academic subjects or Curricular Stream Specific requirement of subjects of study for particular occupation is the basis of this classification. Geographical Files Occupational information can also be filed geographically by city or state Characteristics of a good filing system:

In order to select a filing system for the school, the guidance worker should examine all the classification system available. Then a filing plan needs to be selected suitable to the requirements of the school. Following are the characteristics of a good filing system suggested by (1976, 1.63):

(i) It should provide a safe place for housing written and printed documents, clippings from newspapers and magazines, posters, pictures, films taperecordings, pamplates, books and anything else that may contain useful occupational information.

(ii) It should provide one and only one designated location for each item to be filed, so that there may be no confusion where to file an item or where to find it.

(iii) It should be easy to use, so that all who use it can find what they want with a minimum time and effort.

(iv) It should bring together as many as possible of the materials on any one occupation or industry or employer.

(v) It should bring together related occupations or industries or employers.

(vi) It should provide some means of quickly finding material in omnibus books and other publications which describe several different occupations.

(vii) It should be expandable, so that it can grow as the collection grows.

(viii) It should provide for filing and finding related materials, such as the results of follow up studies and community occupational surveys.

Dissemination of Occupational Information

Dissemination of occupational information about various educational and occupational opportunities and their requirements is necessary to give exposure to students. The dissemination of occupational information helps student to be informed about different careers, to make an appropriate career choice and to apply the information to solve various career related problems. Occupational information can be effectively disseminated to students through group as well as individual techniques.

Group Techniques: In school much of the information on career in general is disseminated through group activities. Group techniques are used in guidance to help the normal individuals to understand themselves, acquire information and learn to analyse problems in order to make realistic educational and vocational choices. Following are some of the group techniques of dissemination of occupational information.

Career Talk: It is a popular technique of dissemination of career information. As per students needs professionals, school alumni can be invited to deliver career talk in regular classroom. The topic of the career talk should be carefully decided keeping in view the age group, interest and educational level. Generally, a career talk contains the following:

(i) Introduction about the occupation,
(ii) General and specific nature of work,
(iii) Work conditions,
(iv) Earnings,
(v) Qualifications required [age, education, skills/aptitude],
(vi) Methods of entering the job,
(vii) Advancement/Promotions,
(viii) Employment outlook,
(ix) Sources of Further information

Group Discussion

In group discussion the group of members share information collected by each one of them and gain insight about a particular occupation. The group discussion should start with prior information to the group about the occupation to be discussed, initiative by group leader, interaction among students [groups] and reflection of discussion.

(a) ***Field Trips:*** Field trips provide a pragmatic, interesting, enjoyable and extremely useful method of learning and imparting occupational information (Joneja, 1997). The students get relevant information about different occupation by visiting industries and offices. While selecting the industry/organisation/place the objective/purpose must be taken into account. Such places may be selected where ex students are working, because they will be able to provide more information and help in making the tour/trip effective. It requires a lot of planning and preparation. After the trip group wise presentation needs to be organised.

(b) ***Career Exhibition:*** It is one of the important techniques of disseminating occupational information. A great variety of career information materials are available from various sources. Exhibition of career information materials may be arranged by the teacher/counselor in the school library, guidance room, hall, and corridor or in classroom or at any other place where all students can see them.

(c) ***School Assemblies:*** School assemblies being a regular feature of secondary and senior secondary schools, can provide opportunities for effective dissemination of occupational information which may be of interest to most of the school students.

(d) ***Subject Teaching:*** There is also scope for dissemination of occupational information in secondary school through subject teaching. In Language, social science, mathematics, science there is maximum scope for diffusion of occupational information. The dissemination of occupational/career information by subject teachers motivate the students to learn the subject matter with interest and to explore further information (NCERT,2008).

(e) ***Publications:*** The educational institution may publish; Guidance Newsletter periodically for teachers and students of the institution.

Individual Techniques: Individual methods of dissemination of occupational information are used to help different types of student to develop an understanding of themselves, and make career related decisions and adjustments. Individual counselling sessions are helpful for dissemination of occupationala. However, as this needs one to one interaction professional expertise is essential on the part of teacher to disseminate career information. Group techniques are more useful and economic.

Job Satisfaction

(a) ***Meaning of Job Satisfaction***: Job satisfaction is a person's attitude towards the job. Positive attitude towards job are equivalent to job satisfaction where as negative attitude are equivalent to job dissatisfaction. Job satisfaction describes how content an individual is with his/her job. The happier people are within their job, the more satisfied they are said to be. Job satisfaction is not the same as motivation, although it is clearly linked. For the first time in 1935, the concept of job satisfaction gained momentum through the publication by Hoppock on job satisfaction. "*Hoppock* in his monograph has defined job satisfaction as any combination of psychological, physiological and environmental circumstances that causes a person truthfully to say I am satisfied with my job". Job satisfaction has been defined as a pleasurable emotional state resulting from the appraisal of one's job (Locke, 1976) an affective reaction to one's job (Cranny, Smith & Stone, 1992) and an attitude towards one's job (Brief, 1998). Weiss (2002) argued that job satisfaction is an attitude but points out that researchers should clearly distinguish the objects of cognitive evaluation which are affect (emotion), beliefs and behaviours. This definition suggests that we form attitudes towards our jobs by taking into account our feelings, our beliefs, and our behaviors. Job satisfaction may also be defined as summation of employee's feelings in four important areas.

(b) ***Factors of Job satisfaction***: Job satisfaction can be influenced by a variety of factors, e.g. the quality of one's relationship with their supervisor, the quality of the physical environment in which they work, degree of fulfillment in their work, etc. Numerous research results show that there are many factors affecting the job satisfaction. There are particular **demographic traits** (age, education level, tenure, position, marital status, years in service, and hours worked per week) of employees that significantly affect their job satisfaction.

Motivating factors are achievement, recognition, the job conducted, responsibility, promotion and the factors related to the job itself for personal development. Motivating factors in the working environment result in the job satisfaction of the person while protective ones dissatisfy him/her.

Maslow connects the creation of the existence of people's sense of satisfaction with the maintenance of the classified needs. These are: physiological needs (eating, drinking, resting, etc.), security needs (pension, health insurance, etc.), the need to love (good relations with the environment, friendship, fellowship, to love and to be loved), need to self-esteem (self-confidence, recognition, adoration, to be given importance, status, etc.) need of self-actualisation (maximisation of the latent [potential] power and capacity, development of abilities, etc). Insufficient education, inability to select qualified workers for the job, lack of communications, lack of job definitions, all affect job satisfaction negatively. It has been asserted that participating in the management, having the decision making power, independence on the job and the unit where the individual works, have positive impact upon the job satisfaction. The job itself (the work conducted), and achievement and recognition at work result in satisfaction while the management policy, relations with the managers and colleagues result in dissatisfaction. Factors related to the job itself such as using talents, creativity, responsibility, recognition have influence on the job satisfaction. Age is one of the factors affecting job satisfaction. Studies conducted in five different countries prove that the elder workers are more satisfied. The role people play and the status they enjoy are all too often determined by age. Besides other things, age is also an important consideration in determining a person's promotion or his/her failure to receive it. Length of service is also a factor affecting job satisfaction. Similarly, by some researchers, sex is also found to have an influence on job satisfaction. Besides, job satisfaction and devotion to the job, affected each other reciprocally, and they have great impact upon performance. The most significant of the factors affecting performance are economical, technical, socio-political, cultural and demographical ones. However, most efforts to improve performance seem to center on improving the conditions surrounding the work. These are worthwhile efforts, but they usually result only in short-term improvements in attitudes and productivity, and the situation often returns quickly to normal.

Job Analysis, Job Specifications and Job Profile

Job Analysis: Job analysis is the process of objectively determining the specific duties, responsibilities and working conditions associated with a specific job, as well as the personal skills and qualifications required to perform that job satisfactorily. It is the process of getting information about the job. Thus, the purpose of job analysis is to establish and document the job relatedness of employment procedures. It investigates exactly:

(i) What the worker does in a particular job?
(ii) How s/he does that particular job?
(iii) Why s/he does it? and
(iv) How much skill is required to do it ?
(v) What are the physical demands, environmental conditions associated with this specific job?

Some of the methods of job analysis are:

(i) Review of job classification system
(ii) Interviews: Incubement interviews and supervisor interview
(iii) Expert panel
(iv) Observation
(v) Incubement work logs

Advantages of Job analysis

(i) Job analysis helps the personnel manager at time of recruitment and selection of right personnel in right job.
(ii) Understanding the extent and scope of training required in the field.
(iii) It helps in chalking out the compensation plan for employees.
(iv) It helps the personnel in performance appraisal of employees.

These may be used individually or in combination. Job analysis can be done in two ways: job description and job specifications.

Job Specifications

Job specification is a statement which tells us minimum acceptable human qualities which helps to perform a job. It helps in selecting an appropriate person for an appropriate position. The components covered under job specifications are:

(i) Job title and designation
(ii) Educational qualification for that title
(iii) Physical and other related attributes
(iv) Mental Health
(v) Special attributes and abilities
(vi) Maturity and dependability
(vii) Relationship of that job with other jobs

Advantages of Job Specifications

(i) It is helpful in preliminary screening in selection procedures
(ii) It helps in giving due justifications to each job
(iii) It helps in designing training and development programmes

(iv) It helps the supervisors for counsellingand monitoring performance of employees

(v) It helps in job evaluation

(vi) It helps the management to take decisions regarding promotions, transfer and giving extra benefits to employees.

Job Profile

Job Profile is a breakdown of the duties and tasks required of and performed by a person for a specific title. Job profile or the Key Result Areas indicate a list of activities that you are doing or will be doing in any job. It defines your job responsibilities (the activities you are autorised to do in any job). Whenever, you wish to switch to new job, your existing and previous experience is counted on the basis of your job profile and that is why job opportunities depend on the job profile. Job profiles list a general description of the work position including required duties, position goals and departmental placement. Also, job profiles list candidate educational and experience requirements. For example, the candidate "must have three years of sales experience." Many job profiles also list the position's salary or hourly wage. A job profile presents a clear picture of the position to the candidate. After reading the job profile, job seekers can make an informed decision as to whether the job is right for them. For applicants, a well-written job profile serves as a valuable interview preparation tool.

10

The Counselling Service

Introduction

In the first unit, you have read about guidance. Sometimes you may be confused about the two terms guidance and counselling. In this unit, we will discuss about the concept of counselling, its meaning, principles and goals. We will also know about the process of counselling and role and functions of a counsellor. Counselling is the central aspect of the whole guidance programme. All the activities and services of the guidance programme leads to and help in the counselling process. Counselling is aimed at helping the individual in solving problems in future and also enhancing personal, social, emotional, educational and vocational development. Counselling has Remedial, Preventive and Developmental value.

Objectives

After reading this unit, students will be able to:

(i) Explain the concept of counselling,
(ii) State the types of counselling,
(iii) Explain the process of counselling,
(iv) Explain the characteristics and skills of counsellor,
(v) Describes the role and functions of a counsellor.

The Concept of Counselling

Counselling the intimate and vital part of entire guidance. *Webster's Dictionary* defines counselling as consultation, mutual interchange of opinions, deliberating together. *Wren says*, counselling is a dynamic and purposeful relationship between two people who approach a mutually defined problem with mutual consideration for each other to the end that the younger or less mature, or more troubled of the two is aided to a self determined resolution of his problem. Counselling helps a person to comes to see who he really is, what he has and does not have, what he can do easily, what he can do with difficulty and what he cannot do at all. It is a close sharing of a human relationship with one who has for him a high regard; one who can offer him unconditional acceptance, but one who has no guarantees, no answers. Counselling is a process that occurs between two individuals...counsellor and counselee (client) It. takes place within a professional setting. It is initiated and maintained as a means of facilitating changes in the behaviour of the client. It is a professional task for professionally trained people.

Meaning of Counselling

Though the term guidance and counselling is used interchangeably, both the terms have different meaning. We have studied about guidance, now we will know about counselling. In everyday life, we find counselling goes on at many levels. In a family, parents counsel their children, doctors counsel patients, lawyers to clients and teachers to students. There is no limitation to the problems or counsellors in providing counselling, so, let us know what counselling is. According to *Webster dictionary* counselling is defined as consultation, mutual interchange of opinions, deliberating together. Counselling is a dynamic and purposeful relationship between two people who approach a mutually defined problem, with mutual consideration of each other to the end that the younger or less mature or more troubled of the two is aided to a self determined resolution to his problem.

(a) **Wren:** Counselling is an interaction process which facilitates meaningful understanding of self and environment and results in the establishment and or clarification of goals and values for future behaviours.

(b) **Shertzer and Stone:** Counselling is an accepting, trusting and safe relationship in which clients learn to discuss openly what worries and upsets them, to define precise behaviour goals, to acquire the essential social skills and to develop the courage and self confidence to implement desired new behaviour.

(c) **Merle M. Ohlsen:** Counselling is a process by which a troubled person (client) is helped to tell and behave in a more personally satisfying manner through interaction with an uninvolved person (counsellor) who provides information and reactions which stimulate the client to develop behaviour which enable him to deal more effectively with himself and his environment.

(d) **Edwin Lewis** -- If all the definitions are analyzed we can come to the following conclusions.

(i) Counselling is a two-way process.
(ii) It involves two individuals.
(iii) There is a mutual relationship between the two individuals.
(iv) It helps an individual to gain self understanding self acceptance and self-realisation.
(v) It helps an individual to become happier more creative and better adjusted.

Let us now discuss what counselling is not. Counselling is a process which included a number of activities like giving information, advice and counselling etc. But it is not an individual activity like giving information/ advice/suggestion/recommendation only. From this it is clear that what is counselling is.

Counselling constitutes the three activities like - I - Informing A-Advising and C - Counselling. **Informing:** Here the role of the counsellor is to give appropriate and correct information to the clients. For example you are a student and you need counselling to select your course for the future. Here the role of the counsellor is to give you information about the availability of different courses & its future prospects. **Advising:** In this stage the counsellor suggests appropriate courses of action. Here the counsellor will offer you several options and recommends one according to your aim or interest. For example if your aim is to be an engineer, the counsellor will suggest you a course related to applied mathematics. **Counselling:** In this stage counsellor helps the students to clarify his needs, feelings or motivations so that he can make the appropriate decision for himself. For example if you will tell, you have no aim or you can not decide what you will do in the future. So, the counsellor will ask you if you are not sure about what to do in future but you must want to do something interesting so describe about your idea. Like this the counsellor can motivate you to find out your idea & can recommend you the course according to your interest.

So, counselling is student dependent rather than knowledge dependent. As a counsellor or a person needs skill rather than knowledge it needs high level of interpersonal skills. So, counselling is a process which constitutes information, advising and counselling. You can think of these three activities as a continuous spectrum of areas which merge into each other.

Characteristics of Counselling

The concept of counselling will be clear to you by knowing it's meaning, characteristics and functions. Counselling involves two individuals - one seeking help and the other, a professionally trained person, who can help the first. There should be a relationship of mutual respect between the two. The counsellor should be friendly and cooperative and the counselee should have trust and confidence in the counsellor. The aim of counselling is to help a student form a decision, make a choice or seek direction. It helps a counselee to acquire independence and develop a sense of responsibility, explore and utilise his potentialities. It is more than advice giving. The progress comes through the thinking that a person with a problem does for himself rather than through solutions offered by the counsellor. Its function is to produce changes in the individual that will enable him to extricate himself from his difficulties. Emotional rather than purely intellectual attitudes are the raw material of the counselling process. It helps an individual to know himself better, gives him confidence, encourages his self-directedness and provides him with new vision to grow.

Functions of Counselling

Like guidance, counselling has also three fold functions adjust mental, oriental and developmental.

(a) ***Adjustmental Functions:*** Rapid social change brought about by industrialisation and urbanisation has led to several perplexing problems. The pace of this change is ever on the increase, thus making adjustment a continuous process of grappling way with new situations. Counselling helps the student in making the best possible adjustment to the current situations be it in educational institution, occupational world, in the home and in the community. Professional and individualised aid is given in making immediate and suitable adjustment at problem points.

(b) ***Oriental function:*** Oriental function means to orient the person about his environmental constraints and resources and her personal constraints and resources by giving information and awareness in problems of career planning, educational programming etc. Awareness of the need to plan in the context of the complexity of the world of work is an essential prerequisite of going through education and preparation for after education. So, oriental function is the important function in the counselling process. It is a link between adjustment and development function. If the person is properly oriented, he can develop his plan properly and adjust suitable with himself and society. **Developmental** function Developmental function means not only to help the students having problems but also to help the students before the problems arise. For example, we are giving vaccination to the child as a preventive measure. Even then when the child suffers from a particular disease we take the help of special doctor to cure it. So, both the processes are coming under health development. Likewise in the counselling process the function of counselling is to prevent emergence and maladjustment and cure the person having maladjustment to adjust with the problem situation. Therefore the development function helps in.

(i) Self-development,
(ii) Self-realisation,
(iii) Development of society, and
(iv) National development.

So, we can say that counselling has not only it's functions towards the individual but to the society and nation also.

Principles of Counselling

We have already discussed the meaning and principles of guidance. Now we will discuss the principles of counselling. The principles on which the process of counselling is based are:

(i) It involves a face-to-face relationship between two persons.
(ii) It is emotional rather than purely intellectual attitude.
(iii) It is more than advice giving. The progress comes through the thinking that a person with a problem does for himself.
(iv) It involves solution of immediate problem as well as the future decision of the individual.

The counsellor should follow the above principles while counselling to make the process of counselling effective. It is not an easy task. To make the process successful the counsellor should also follow certain principles in his own self to develop his skills. He should follow the principles as given below during counselling.

(a) ***Warmth:*** The counsellor should communicate personal warmth and make the client feel welcome valued as individuals. Acceptance: The counsellor should accept the person and his feelings for what he is without criticising him. He should also accept the person irrespective of age, race, sex, etc.
(b) ***Genuineness:*** The counsellor should be very honest with himself and with client he should be very open, friendly and undefensive.
(c) ***Empathy:*** Instead of showing sympathy to the person having problem, the counsellor should show empathy, which means to sense the feelings and experience of another person.

In order to make good relationship the above qualities should be acquired by a counsellor. He should imbibe these qualities to follow the principles of counselling properly.

Goals of Counselling: Welcome to the counsellor's Cabin:

When you enter – The Cabin you will be greeted by a warm and friendly atmosphere that invites you – Come on in and make yourself at home.

Prominently, displayed a copy of the serenity prayer which serves as both counselling mantra and mission statement.

It reads as follows

God grant me the serenity to accept the things i cannot change, courage to change the things I can, and wisdom to know the difference.

Serenity is an acronym use to explain the major components of counselling program to help you determine if you would benefit from engaging in this process.

Spirituality-associated with wholeness/wellness; a sense of meaning/purpose.

Evaluation - assess the problem by taking it apart and putting it back together.

Relationships-Your relationships define and represent who you are.

Emotions - What are you feeling right now? It's important to know. *Needs* - Identify your needs; they are directly related to what you are feeling. *Interpersonal skills* - Life is a series of conversations. What is you style? Treatment - Your personal plan of thinking, feeling, and acting differently. You - Since you are the expert on you, you are the key to your success. As a counsellor you should focus on wellness and personal growth and work extensively on helping people to enhance the quality of their relationships. Many of clients are in search of meaning and direction in various life settings including school, family, and career… all of which involve relationships. Empowerment over life comes through thinking clearly and making wise choices. Unfortunately, problems can become so overwhelming it is difficult to accomplish either one of these. Counselling will equip you with life strategies to help you think, feel, and act differently in order to enhance the quality of your life. If you read the above statements of Dr. Sacky's Cabin, one of the counsellor's cabin you will understand the goals of counselling. The acronym serenity is the goals of counselling.

The Types of Counselling

Based on the nature of the counselling process and the role of the counsellor, the following are the three types of counselling:

Types of Counselling

(A) Directive counselling; — (William son)
(B) Non-directive counselling; — Carl Rogers)
(C) Eclectic counselling — Bordin

(A) Directive Counselling

(i) B. G. Williamson is the chief exponent.
(ii) The counsellor assumes the major responsibility of solving the problem.
(iii) Counsellor identifies, defines, diagnoses and provides a solution to the problem.
(iv) Counsellor directs thinking by informing explaining, interpreting and advising.
(v) Counsellor-oriented.
(vi) Emphasis is on the problem.

Steps: Role of the Counsellor

(a) ***Analysis*:** collecting data from various sources to understand the client's problem.
(b) ***Synthesis*:** interpreting and organizing data to reveal students assets, liabilities, adjustments etc.
(c) ***Diagnosis*:** Identifying the nature and cause of the problem.
(d) ***Prognosis*:** Predicting the future development of the problem.
(e) ***Counselling*:** Taking steps to bring about adjustment.;

(f) ***Follow up*:** Helping with recurrence or new patterns.

Merits

(i) Time saving and economical,
(ii) Gives happiness to the counselee as he gets a solution to this problem.
(iii) Emphasis is on the intellectual rather than the emotional aspect.

Demerits

(i) Kills the initiative,
(ii) Makes him helpless,
(iii) Does not guide counselee to be efficient and confident,
(iv) Undemocratic,
(v) Made dependent

(B) Non-directive Counselling (Client-oriented/Centered Counselling):

(i) Chief exponent - Carl Rogers
(ii) Counselee is allowed free expression
(iii) Counsellor only directs and guides
(iv) Counsellor asks a few questions, so as to think about the solution of the problem.
(v) Counselee takes active part, gains insight into the problem with the help of the counsellor and arrives at the decision and action to be taken.
(vi) Counsellor's role is passive
(vii) Goal is independent and integration of the client rather than the solution.
(viii) Role of the counsellor is to create an atmosphere in which the counselee can work out his own understanding.
(ix) Emotional aspect rather than the intellectual aspect is stressed.
(x) Counselling relationship is the establishment of a warm, permissive and accepting climate which helps the client to express his self structure.

Merits

(i) Freedom of the individual

(ii) Relieves tensions due to catharsis
(iii) Moves toward acceptance of himself
(iv) Confronts weaknesses without feeling threatened

Demerits

(i) Time consuming
(ii) Wisdom and judgement of the client cannot be relied upon
(iii) All the problems cannot be sorted out through talking

(C) Eclectic Counselling

(i) Chief exponent - Bordin (Thome).
(ii) Counselling may be evaluated along a continuum from directive to non directive to directive.
(iii) Eclectic is a continuation and synthesis of directive and non-directive counselling.
(iv) Both counsellor and counselee are active and co-operative.
(v) Both do the talking in turn.
(vi) The problem is solved jointly.

The counsellor studies the needs and personality of the client and then selects the technique (appropriate). Begins with directive but switches over to non-directive or vice versa as demanded by the situation.

Steps

(i) Initial interview
(ii) Develops rapport and does structuring so that client understands what to expect from the counselling.
(iii) Tentative diagnosis and plan of counselling is formulated.
(iv) Gathers information about the client and the client needs to be helped to assimilate this information.
(v) Client achieves emotional release and gains insights, modifies perceptions/attitudes about himself and situations.

On-Line Counselling

On-line counselling refers to the provision of professional mental health counselling services concerns via the internet. Services are typically offered via email, real time chat and video conferencing. Some clients' use online counselling in conjunction with traditional psycho-therapy, and others use it as an occasional check-in tool for their lives. **On-line Counselling:** On-line counselling is simply communicating with a qualified, professional counsellor/therapist by email or chat through your computer, instead of having to make a visit to your counsellor's office; you can receive the same professional care in the comfort of your own home. If you have a microphone, we can speak to each other through the computer. Whether you choose only a few email exchanges or on ongoing dialogue with the counsellor over time, you have the opportunity to share your concerns, pose questions, and gain further insight into the problems you are addressing. Advantages of using On-line Counselling

(i) Convenient - any time, any place, whatever suits you.
(ii) Flexible - you control everything; receive help when you want it.
(iii) Can deal with embarrassing issues without having to see anyone.
(iv) Your anonymity is protected.
(v) Get to the root of the problem quicker as writing lets you get in touch with your feelings.
(vi) More cost and time effective as you can deal with more issues in a session.
(vii) No need to take time off work.
(viii) Receive specialised help no matter where you live in the world.

Why Choose on-line counselling?

(i) Easy access to a professional counsellor or therapist though email or live chat.
(ii) Select an experienced professional from many qualified to deal with your problem.
(iii) You can select a counsellor who lives anywhere in the world.
(iv) ***Convenience*** - takes place in your home or wherever you are twenty four hours a day seven days a week.
(v) Cheaper than regular counselling.
(vi) Anonymity and security.

(vii) ***Flexibility*** - either you can get quick answers or guidance to problems or you can schedule regular sessions

Live Chat the first few minutes of all live chat sessions are completely free of charge. Since payment starts only when you choose to hire the counsellor, you have the opportunity to discuss you questions and/or concerns, negotiate a price that suits your budget and ensure that you feel comfortable with this specific counsellor.

E-mail: Email counselling is another form of online counselling that may suit your needs.

(i) You may find that expressing concerns and questions in writing helps organise and focus on your problem.
(ii) It is an extremely convenient way for you to communicate with a counsellor. The benefits of on-line counselling with live person
(iii) Liveperson is one of the best and most well known online counselling specialists.
(iv) You will have an enormous choice of professionals you can seek help from - (experts in over 600 categories).
(v) You will find Liveperson very user-friendly.
(vi) You can consuit with professionals in real time via live chat and email.
(vii) You will find Liveperson is reliable, very easy to use and enables you to get instant answers to your most urgent questions.
(viii) I full recommend this service to you because so many people have benefited from it click now to get started.

Disadvantages of Counselling or Therapy by E-mail:

Remote counselling via e-mail carries many disadvantages as well as advantages in comparison to traditional, face-to-face counselling.

Communication and the Counselling Relationship

Communicating only introduces particular challenges for creating and sustaining a working relationship. Lack of Visual and Verbal Cues It can be difficult enough to understand exactly what someone is saying in a face-to-face setting, but stripped of the kinds of visual and auditory verbal cues which we take for granted when communicating in person the struggle to understand takes on a whole new dimension. Part of the beauty of the English Language is that the same statement can take on a whole range of subtle meanings: but without that grin or frown that raised eyebrow, that softened voice or dead-pan delivery, figuring out which meaning a person intends can be a real challenge. The lack of visual cues is also especially important for clients who would like to discuss a visible physical disability and would like their counsellor to be able to see exactly what they are talking about.

Lack of Physical Presence: The lack of a physical presence of another person in the same room may make some people feel less emotionally intimate and less comforted in times of distress.

Asynchronous Nature of E-mail: It can be frustrating to have to wait for the counsellor to reply when using email and other forms of communication that are asynchronous (meaning that two people are writing at different times, as opposed to conversing in real time). Urgency in a similar vein, the inevitable time delay associated with email exchanges precludes the kind of urgent attention (or even emergency response) which is possible in a face-to-face setting.

No Regular Appointment Times

Just as the freedom to work without fixed appointment times can be an advantage for some clients, the absence of the structure which fixed appointments provide can be a disadvantage for others. Many clients prefer the structure of having to attend a session at the same time every week.

Computer concerns

Relying on computers as a communications medium can bring technology into the foreground of the counselling process as an unwelcome participant.

Equipment and Internet Service Failures Hardware or software failure or internet service failure can impact the online availability of both counsellor and client. Ideally, the technology becomes transparent', so it simply serves as a tool for communication, without requiring attention in and of itself. In practice, however, even the best technological tools sometimes require attention, and it can be frustrating it this occurs during a counselling exchange. Confidentiality and Privacy in Shared Environments Using computers at work, in an internet cafe or public library, or any other environment where other people have access to the same equipment introduces particular pitfalls for confidentiality and privacy in email counselling.

Of course, there are things that the face to face counselling covers that the e-therapy lacks. We are talking of the Non-verbal communication that is missing when the screen separates people. Also, it may happen that a person needs to be physically comforted when being in a counselling session and we can not do that on-line. Being aware of those disadvantages, we as professionals, face our role with all our heart and seriousness so as to make the best out of all the strengths of the online counselling.

The Process of Counselling

Counselling is a process: It means that counselling involves a sequence of identifiable events spread over a period of time. The time taken, the sequence of events, and dynamics involved, the nature and extent of exploration, differ from individual to individual. However, there are certain basic stages, which form the essentials of counselling processes. The process of counselling comprises of certain concepts, they are as follows:

Readiness: The counselee are of two types i.e. one who seeks assistance voluntarily and the other who are referred. The counselling presupposes a desire on the part of the counselee that makes him come for the assistance. This desire is referred to as readiness.

Counter Will: People experience difficulty in asking for help and accepting it, because they are reluctant to face the consequences of change or an admission of inadequacy of failure. The negative feeling that holds back one from seeking help is referred to, as counter will.

Case History: Case History is a systematic collection of facts about the counselee's past and present life. However, focus of attention varies from case to case.

Rapport: It is a warm friendly and understanding atmosphere created by the counsellor, which is catalytical in the formation of an effective counselling relationship. Warmth of relationship and feeling of trust, which grows out of unconditional acceptance are important in contributing to the establishment of rapport.

Transference: It refers to the counsellor transferring amotions originally felt toward someone early in life. The counselee is encouraged to express his/her feelings and emotions freely. The counsellor acknowledges these feelings and handles in a therapeutic way.

***Counter Transference*:** This occurs when counsellor project their unresolved conflicts upon the counselee. When counsellor feels uncomfortable and experience feelings of anger, resentment or become overemotional. This is unhealthy.

Resistance: It refers to counselee's move to oppose the counsellor's attempt to work towards set goals. This influences counselling outcome positively. Resistance ranges from open hostility to passively resistant behaviour like being late for an appointment.

Stages of the Counselling Process

A process is an identifiable sequence of events taking place over time e.g. Process of human development from birth to death.

The First Stage: Initial Disclosure: Initially the client expresses two sets of feelings i.e., (a) I know I need help; (b) I wish I weren't here.

(i) Therefore central task of the counsellor in this stage is to allay the client's fears and encourage self-disclosure.
(ii) Attending paying careful attention to the client's words and actions.

Counsellor observes clients behaviour for indications of content and feeling not expressed in verbal message. It is the first contact between the client and the counsellor, but it remains important throughout the counselling process. In this stage, clients are helped to articulate their personal concerns and to place those concerns in a context so that the counsellor can understand the personal meanings and significance the client attaches to them. The main aim of this stage is promote trust in the client. Following characteristics describe the helping relationship.

- ***Empathy*** - Understanding others experience as if it were yours.
- ***Genuineness*** - Being natural, consistent in behavior and dependable in the relationship.
- ***Unconditional positive regard*** - Caring without condition.
- ***Concreteness*** - Using clear language to describe the client's situation.

The Second Stage: In-depth Exploration client begins to formulate a new sense of hope and direction.

- Counsellor at first discusses the diagnostic impressions of the client's dynamic and coping behaviour.
- As the relationship becomes more secure, the counsellor begins to confront the client with observations about his/her goals or behaviour. This will help the client arrive at newly challenged and refined views of self.
- Immediacy - is referred to in three ways.

(i) General discussions about the progress of counselling relationship.

(ii) Immediate response to the client's statement disclosing current thoughts about counselling.

(iii) Counsellor's personal response to a client in the present. This stage becomes emotionally stressful, because client faces the inadequacy of habitual behaviours. In this stage client and counsellor come to a mutually acceptable diagnosis of the problem.

The Third Stage: commitment to Action: How to accomplish goals that have emerged in the previous two stages. Client relates his behaviour to accomplish goals. This stage includes identifying possible alternative courses of actions (decisions) the client might choose. Once an action decision is made the client tries some new behaviors. The counsellor supports and reinforces the trying of new behaviours.

The Skills of Counselling

(i) ***Listening*:** It is the process of hearing the other person. (a) During listening it is important to show that the counsellor is listening through the minimal prompts' such as head nods, yes, no etc. They indicate that I am with you.

Overuse of these should be avoided. (b) Behavioural aspects of listening - (Soler) S - Sit squarely; O – Openness; L – Leaning; E - Eye contact; R - Relax Aspects of Listening Linguistic aspects - words, phrases, figures of speech.

(b) ***Paralinguistic aspects*:** timing, volume, tone pitch, ums' and errs', fluency non-verbal aspects: facial expression, gestures, touch, body position, and proximity to the counsellor, body movement and eye contact. Attending and showing receptiveness. It is the act of truly focusing on the other person. It involves consciously making ourselves aware of what the other person is saying and of what they are trying to communicate to us.

(c) ***Observing Body Messages:*** Non-verbal aspects of communication refer to body language. The way the client expresses through the use of their body. They offer clues about the client's internal status beyond the words.

Morris calls it Man Watching. Body language depends on context in which it occurs, the nature of the relationship, individual's personal style, personality of the person. Therefore, avoid assuming what person is saying with their body languages.

(i) ***Attraction*:** Attention is focused on what you are feeling rather than what client is saying.

(ii) ***Physical condition*:** Sick/tired, without realizing it you tune out certain things client is saying.

(iii) ***Concerns*:** Preoccupied with you own concerns.

(iv) ***Over-eagerness*:** Listen to only a part and respond.

(v) ***Similarity of Problems*:** Same as your own problem. Your mind wanders.

(vi) ***Differences*:** Different experiences of yours and client.

(vii) ***Distracting:*** Effective Listening:

(viii) Attention focusses outward,

(ix) Suspension of judgement,
(x) Attention to the behavioral aspects (Soler),
(xi) Avoidance of interpretation,
(xii) Development of free-floating attention.

Communicating

It is the exchange of ideas and opinions between two or more people through speech, writing or signs. The communication included physical setting as well as psychological predispositions of the receiver. Communication = thoughts and feelings.

Factors Involved in the Communication

(i) Purpose: Specific
(ii) Distribution
(iii) Environment
(iv) Timing
(v) Feedback
(vi) Follow-up

Causes of Communication Breakdown

(i) Lack of consideration of the other person's feelings and personality;
(ii) Use of technical language;
(iii) Not thinking about other, how they get affected (networking missing);
(iv) Lose human factor (envy, jealousy).

Clarification: To get definite information through this to help clarify the client's thinking without pressurising.

Concreteness: Using clear language to describe the client's life situation. It promotes clear insight in client's life and provides counsellor with a fuller sense of the uniqueness of the client's experiences.

Restatement: Enables the counsellor to let the counselee realise that he is being fully understood and accepted. Counsellor exactly repeats as said by the client. Client thus gets a rest and a chance to collect his thoughts before going forward.

Paraphrasing: The counsellor summarises. He chooses/selects those ideas and feelings which seem most important and relevant and feeds them back to the client in a more organised form.

Ways to Impede Communication

(i) Counsellor's predispositions,
(ii) Premature advice giving,
(iii) Lecturing,
(iv) Excessive questioning,
(v) Story telling

Questioning

What it is? Questions are used to draw out information from others. *How to use it?* There are several types of question. Choose the most appropriate: *Open-ended questions*: Open questions promote discovery and stimulate thinking. They are useful to help the other person to start talking about a topic, outline a situation, and give a broad description of what happened and how he or she reacted. There are three broad types of open question.

Clarifying question

(i) What specifically does that mean to you?
(ii) Can I make sure I understand that…?
(iii) If I hear correctly, what you are saying is…?

Creative questions

(i) How have you seen others handle similar situations?
(ii) What do you think about…?
(iii) Would you like to talk more about it?
(iv) I'd be interested in hearing more?
(v) What would be your approach if there were no constraints?

Process questions

(i) What would you like to get from this session?
(ii) What do I need to communicate to ensure everyone understands your role?

(iii) What authority do you think you need to complete this task?

Follow-up or probing questions, the purpose of follow-up questions is to get information, broaden decisions and understand reasons and motivations. Do not over use why'. It causes people to become defensive.

(i) In what way would this to achieve greater customer satisfaction?
(ii) What other aspects of this should be considered?
(iii) How would you involve others in accomplishing this plan?

Follow-up questions are useful for probing - getting to the heart of a topic, checking information and filling in detail. A particular type of follow-up question is the reflective question, useful for gaining a clearer understanding, revealing more information or uncovering feelings.

(i) You say you were pleased....
(ii) Incompetent....
(iii) You say he reacted to this. How did he react....?

Closed questions: Closed questions are those that lead to either yes or no. They are useful in checking facts quickly but can lead to a one-sided conversation.

Examples are:

(i) Have you been shopping recently?
(ii) Is there enough money in the bank?
(iii) Have you done this sort of work before?

A closed question can be useful lead into open questions once an area to explore has been identified. Less useful questions. Certain types of questions are less useful. Try not to use them - these include: Leading questions (I assume you...) Hypothetical questions (If you were in my place....) Multiple questions.

Characteristics and Skills of a Counsellor

A good counsellor should be:

(i) A good listener and good communicator;
(ii) Respectful to other person's feelings and point of view;
(iii) Kind, caring and understanding;
(iv) Non-judgemental;
(v) Trustworthy and respectful of people's confidentiality;
(vi) Relaxed and calm;
(vii) Warm and approachable;
(viii) The ability to motivate and inspire clients.

Role and Functions of Counsellor

Counsellor is a specialist in education. Counsellor's responsibilities can be classified into (a) Diagnostic, (b) therapeutic (c) Evaluation and Research with specialised services and skills. A counsellor is selected by virtue of interest, training, experience and competence. The specific functions of a counsellor are:

(i) Orientation of students,
(ii) Student appraisal,
(iii) Educational and occupational information service,
(iv) Holding counselling interviews,
(v) Placement,
(vi) Research and Evaluation.

The Counsellor: Design and initiate a comprehensive career development programme involve teachers, students, parents, community resources. Plans students competencies for use in the classroom include para professionals Assist students in career selection, prepare them and progress in it. The counsellor acts as a facilitator.

The counsellor needs to keep up-to-date information regarding new career trends and to participate in professional experiences to improve their skills.

11

Counselling Approaches

Introduction

In the previous chapter, you have studied about the concept of counselling, types of counselling and the role and functions of a counsellor. You may observe that the perspective of counselling changes from counsellor to counsellor. There are differences in training, clients and settings and even goals. But the basic perspective of counselling remains the same with different emphasis. Along with differences it is worth to note the commonalites. Common to all these perspectives are the notions that:

(i) Counselling is aimed at helping people make choices and act on them.
(ii) Counselling is a learning process, and
(iii) Counselling enables personality development.

Therefore, prospective counselors should be aware of major approaches to counselling so as to enable them to acquire a sound basis for developing their own personal brand of counselling. The current trends in this area are broadly classified into three approaches.

They are: Cognitive approaches, Affective approaches, and Behavioural approaches.

The approaches are closely paraller with the three aspects of personality — cognition, affection and co-nation i.e., knowing, feeling and doing. In this unit, we will discuss the cognitive and affective approaches to counselling.

Objectives

After reading this unit you will be able to:

(i) State the approaches to counselling;
(ii) Explain cognitive oriented counselling approach and afftective oriented counselling approach;
(iii) Describe the factors influencing counselling;
(iv) Discuss the legal and ethical considerations in counselling

Cognitively Oriented Counselling Approaches

Cognitive Approaches: As *Feorge and Cristiani (1981)* have pointed out, in the cognitive approaches, the process of counselling is the curing of unreason by reason; i.e., to help clients eliminate most emotional disturbances by learning to think rationally, to help them get rid of illogical, irrational ideas and attitudes and substitute logical, rational ideas and attitudes. It is believed that this process helps the client to attain rational behaviour, happiness, and self-actualisation.

For example, Transactional Analysis (TA) aims at the internal dialogues of individuals, which occurs between:

(a) Counselling is aimed at helping people make choices and act on them;
(b) Counselling is a learning process, and;
(c) Counselling enables personality development.

A recent and much accepted definition is: Counselling denotes a professional relationship between a trained counselor and client. This relationship is usually person-to-person, although it may sometimes involve more than two people. It is designed to help clients to understand and their selfdetermined goals through meaningful resolution of problems of an emotional or interpersonal nature *(Burks and Stefflre, 1979)*. The merit of the definition by Burks and Steffler is that it is sufficiently theoretilcal and at the same time reasonably operational.

Theory and Practice of Counselling: Theory and practice should go hand in hand. Many trained counselors initially adhere to the theory while starting their career as counsellor. However, even those who are fanatically tied down to one theory appear to change over time. This is because, the client is a human being and he is the link between the theory and practice of the counsellor. Rigid theories, like the Procrustean bed, repel the human psyche. When the man does not fit into the theory the counsellor it's compelled to change his theory. This is one of the most demanding challenges of counselling. Counsellors should keep their minds more receptive and flexible. The psychological concept of individual difference must be understood thoroughly. Individual clients differing in their personalities come with dissimilar problems, goals and aspirations. To believe that all those clients would benefit from one kind of theory is unrealistic. It is useful to know that all the well-known theories have emerged from the practice of individual counsellor's personal experience with counseles. This is why we have different theories and practices. Trying to know theories as old and new broadens our perspective. But what would be ultimately useful is the one that is carved out from the counselor's experience with the various ego states and the struggles between the real parts of their behaviour (whether the same is productive or counter productive) and the behaviour of others by identifying which ego state is in power at any given time.

TA thus gives the clients information about the various types of transactions that occur among individuals and to help them identify the kinds of behavior in which they are involved. The goal of TA is to help clients review their past decisions and make new decisions about their present behaviour. It is assumed that this would change their life direction into developing an autonomous life style characterised by awareness, spontaneity. This, it s believed that would, eliminate a life style characterised by manipulative game- playing a self- defeating neurotic tendencies.

Directive teaching is the core in all the cognitive approaches. For example in *Rational Emotive Therapy (RET)* the counseollor takes up an active teaching role to educate clients. The RET counsellor makes the client understand that the latter's internationalised sentences are quite illogical and especially the current illogical thinking are self-defeating verbalisations of the client. The success if the counselor lies in bringing illogical thinking forcefully to the client's attention. He must also show to the counselee how these thoughts are maintaining his unhappiness and how a rethinking and maintenance of logically and rationality make him happy and contented. In reality therapy, the meaning of reality and the necessity to act responsibly are taught by the counselor.

***Trait and Factor Oriented counselling approaches*:** The trait-factor approach has developed from a marriage of differential psychology's research and theories to Parson's vocational guidance concepts. The approach was born at the *Minnesota Employment Stabilisation Research* Institute and the University of Minnesota Test Bureau as a practical response to educational and vocational adjustment problems of the unemployed and students. It is still closely identified with educational and vocational counseling. The approach has placed heavy reliance on the scientific method by attempting systematically to observe and measure individuals. Traits are categories that are used for describing individual differences in behavior, and statistical methods of factor analysis are used to ascertain how many factors are sufficient to account for similarities and difference in individuals. Trait-factorists have relied heavily on empirical objective data for a logical problem–solving approach to client problems. Thus, the approach may be placed in the constellation of theories that are more cognitively than affectively oriented. Its basic model of analysis, synthesis, diagnosis, prognosis, counseling, and follow-up is a structured, stepwise attempt to help the client become self-counseled. The major component of the model is the integration of objective test data with client subjective data to arrive at a differential diagnosis.

As it has evolved, the trait-factor approach has become more developmental, dynamic, process-oriented, and eclectic. It has moved to a person times environment fit approach, which is seen not as static but as reciprocal and dynamic *(Martin and Swartz-Kulstad, 2000)*. Vocational counselling, in particular, is not seen as fixed but as a continuing experience with definable stages. The contemporary approach is eclectic in that it sees merit and utility in cognitive therapies such as the reality, rational-emotive, and behavioral approach is eclectic in that it sees merit and utility in cognitive therapies such as the reality, rational-emotive, and behavioural approaches. The logical basis of the approach relies heavily on a mentoring and teaching role by the counselor to influence and change the irrational thinking and behavior of the client. A great deal of knowledge, experience, and expertise is assumed of the counselor. Trait-factor counselling is most commonly founding school, employment, and rehabilitation counseling. By including a broader diagnostic scheme, more advanced information-processing concepts, and a more adaptive counselling style, the person times environment fit approach has matured beyond the old trait-factor model. The person time's environment model includes these elements by organising personal constructs, the world of work, person time's environment interactions and then applying them in a problem-solving sequence. Including current concepts of problem solving, information processing, and attitude change has *reinvigorated* a venerable approach to career counselling(Chartrand, 1991).

Frank Parsons' Trait and Factor Theory of Occupational Choice: People perform best when they are in jobs best suited to their abilities Frank parsons are regarded as the founder of the vocational guidance movement. He developed the talent- matching approach, which was later developed into the Trait and Factor Theory of Occupational Choice. At the centre of Parsons' theory is the concept of matching. He states that occupational decision making occurs when people have achieved.

(i) An accurate understanding of their individual traits (aptitudes, interests, personal abilities);
(ii) A knowledge of jobs and the labour market;
(iii) Rational and objective judgement about the relationship between their individual traits, and the labour market.

This three-part theory still governs most current practice. The trait and factor theory operates under the premise that it is possible to measure both individual talents and the attributes required in particular jobs. It also assumes that people may be matched to an occupation that's a good fit. Parsons suggests that when individuals are in jobs best suited to their abilities they perform best and their productivity is highest.

In his book, choosing a Vocation Parsons maintains that personal counsel is fundamental to the career search. In particular, he notes seven stages for a career counsellor to work through with clients:

(a) ***Personal data:*** Create a statement of key facts about the person, remembering to include every fact that has bearing on the vocational problem.
(b) ***Self-analysis:*** Self-examination is done in private and under the instruction of the counsellor. Every tendency and interest that might impact on the choice of a life work should be recorded.
(c) ***The client's own choice and decision:*** This may show itself in the first two stages. The counsellor must bear in mind that the choice of vocation should be made by the client, with the counsellor acting as guide.
(d) ***Counsellor's analysis:*** The counsellor tests the client's decision to see if it is in line with the main quest.
(e) ***Outlook on the vocational field:*** The counsellor should be familiar with industrial knowledge such as lists and classifications of industries and vocations, in addition to locations of training and apprenticeships.
(f) ***Induction and advice:*** Broad-minded attitudes coupled with logical and clear reasoning are critical at this stage.
(g) ***General helpfulness:*** The counsellor helps the client to fit into the chosen work, and to reflect on the decision. Much of Parsons work still guides career counselling today, though it is not without criticism. Matching assumes a degree of stability within the labour market. However, the reality is that the markets volatility means individuals must be prepared to change and adapt to their circumstances.

It has been criticised for being overly cognitive and reductionistic. That is, relying on objective measurements of traits may lead to an over-simplified view of the human condition. Further, the very existence of valid and reliable objective tests, and of stable traits, remains highly questionable. Trait-factor counsellingis also limited insofar as it only seeks to describe a client's potential rather than help him achieve it.

E.G. Williamson (1965) was the only trait-factor theorist to address this question: He argued that the counsellor has the responsibility to promote the self-actualisation of his client, rather than just measuring it. Behavioural therapy, like trait-factor counseling, is firmly grounded in the scientific method, and it is committed to bringing experimental findings into clinical practice in order to change clients'behaviour and resolve personal and social problems (Corey, 1986). Behaviorism has its roots in Pavlov's (1927). Trait-factor counsellingis the only counselling method which has its root in vocational counseling. It dates back to 1908, when Frank Parsons founded the Boston Vocational Bureau and stated his conviction that in order to choose the best career, one had to understand oneself, the characteristics of different job environments, and the relationship between these variables. Trait-factor theory was further developed during the testing movement in the US during the 1930's by psychologists like EG Williamson, John Darley, and Donald G. Paterson (Downing, 1975). Trait-factor counselling is an extremely cognitive approach based on the scientific method and the theory of individual differences. Its major underlying assumptions include the following:

(i) Each person has a unique pattern of traits (i.e., interests, abilities, and characteristics) that are relatively stable and rarely change after adolescence.

(ii) These traits are measurable.

Affectively Oriented Counselling Approaches

As the term suggests the affective approaches in counselling focus their attention to what is going on inside the individual, and particularly what the individual is experiencing at a given time. Client-centered counselling of Rogers is perhaps the most well-defined technique in the affective approaches. It also highlights an issue in counselling; namely, how much responsibility can be placed on the clients for their own problem solving?

Rogers believed that when the individual perceived himself as behaving in manner consistent with his picture of himself, he generally experiences feelings of adequacy, security, and worth. If on the other hand, he acts in a manner different from the way he defines himself, he experiences what is known as threat and feels insecure, inadequate, or worthless. Under pressure and with no other alternative, he may then defend himself against this threat using one or more of the commonly described defense mechanisms. Unless counselling eliminates this defensive chain reaction and strengthens his self-concept, the defensive behaviour would increase vulnerability to further threat, guilt, thereby creating more distortion and more self-defeating mechanisms. The role of the therapist is not just eliminating the defense mechanisms. Rogers highlights the importance of congruence. It means the close-matching of awareness and experience. In this context, the client centered counselors emphasises the importance of accurate communication. If a client is aware of communicating a feeling which he is genuinely experiencing, his behavior is said to be congruent or integrated. In incongruent communication the awareness and experience of the client are two different if not opposing things.

So, also the recipient may experience an awareness of phony communication. The implication here for the counselor is that the counselor should help client to face courageously the incongruence between awareness and experience so that communication of his real experiences is in full awareness and not distorted with defense mechanisms and neurotic constrictions.

The self-theory of Rogers also assumes a perspective called phenomenology. According to this perspective, people's reality is that which they perceive. The way to understand individuals is to infer the phenomenological field from their behavior. In other words, the internal frame of reference of the client is used in counselling with the implication that counselors must attempt to perceive client's perceptual worlds as closely as they can. This is known as the empathic skill of the counselor. Individual client's need to strive for wholeness is the focus in Gestalt therapy and counseling. This school of counselling gives importance to the internal world of the individual. Striving for the gestalt or the wholeness is actually a striving for an integration of thinking, feeling, and behaving. The key concept here is awareness. It is believed that the counselors help the clients work toward a total awareness of his experiences. Gestalt psychologists point out that such awareness permits self-regulation and self- control in the direction of increased integration and creativity.

Recently, one of the major forces that have come to occupy an important place in psychology is Existentialism'. Unlike Psychoanalysis, existentialism is a temperamental way of looking at life. It is basically a philosophy of experiences which need not necessarily be categorised into cognitive compartments. Man is essentially an emotional being rather than a rational animal! The existence of man is unique because he is the only being who reacts to the fact of his existence. The awareness of one's own existence and the possibility of non-existence alters the inner world or the phenomenology. These new premises create new experiences and needs that are yet to be known. The predicament of human beings is such that it includes the individual's capacity for increased self- awareness, the search for unique meaning in a meaningless world, being alone and being in relation with others, freedom to choose one's fate, responsibility, anxiety, finiteness and death, and a basic urge for self-actualisation. As a theory existentialism is sound and appealing, but the practice of counselling on the basis of this theory is difficult. However, the existential counselor tries to understand the client as a being and as a being in the world counsellors are supposed to expose his own inner reality and at the same time be human. This according to existentialists enables clients to become aware of similar conditions and qualities in themselves. It is pointed out that through his process clients come to recognise their potentialities and achieve self-growth by accepting it as their responsibility.

In a nut shell, it can be said that making the client accept responsibility for him selfish the aim of existential counselling. The three basic approaches (Cognitive, Affective, and Conative) with their differing foundations vary in their theory and practice of counselling.

By about *1973, Patterson* began to think in terms of commonalities among the approaches. Fortunately, most of the controversies existed only as academic gymnastics at a theoretical level. The practicing counsellors were undergoing transformation as the clients were not interested in theories and their subtleties but were interested only in immediate problem solving. This demand of the client to the counsellor had made many counselors to abandon their dogmatic approach. Orientation of the counselors started changing towards a pragmatic approach. The client and his needs became more important than the counselor's theory and dogma. This was how personal theory emerged. Here, it is absolutely necessary to point out that training in some known approach is better than no training.

Corey (1977), recommends the eclectic approach as a framework to begin with. However, George and *Cristiani (1981)*, point out that although beginning counsellors need a firm understanding of all the major approaches, they should start first with a thorough grounding in one theoretical approach to counselling. It is further pointed out that judicious integration and assimilation of techniques from other approaches could be done with experience.

Psycho-analytic Approach to Counselling

The original so-called taking therapy involves analysing the root causes of behaviour and feelings by exploring the unconscious mind and the conscious mind and relation of it. Many theories and therapies have evolved from the original Freudian psychoanalysis which utilises free association, dreams and transference, as well other strategies to help the client know the functions of their own minds.

Psychoanalysis was developed in the late nineteenth century by *Sigmund* Frued. His therapy explores the dynamic workings of a mind understood to consist of three parts. The hedonistic id, the rational ego and the moral superego, Frued maintained that the condition of the unconscious mind is profoundly influenced by childhood experiences. So, in addition to dealing with the defense mechanisms used by an overburdened ego, his therapy addresses fixations and other issues by probing deeply into client's youth.

Psychoanalysis has three main components:

(i) A method of investigation of the mind and the way one thinks.
(ii) A systematised set of theories about human behaviour.
(iii) A method of treatment of psychological or emotional illness.

Under the broad umbrella of psychoanalysis, there are at least twenty two theoritical orientations regarding human *mentation* and development. The various approaches in treatment called psychoanalysis vary as much as the theories do. The term also refers to a method of studying child development.

Psycho-analytical counselling is concerned with how we deceive ourselves as to our intentions, desires and beliefs and how these deceptions creates conflict between our expressed goals and our actions. It also gives rises to psychodynamic counselling. The term psychodynamic means pertaining to the laws of mental action and its use pre-supposes that there are some principles that determine the relationship between mind and action and that these can be formulated as a basis for therapeutic intervention.

Traditionally, the principles underlying psycho-dynamic counselling as presented as derivations of the psycho-analytic school, founded by Sigmund Fend. But current psycho-dynamic counselling draws from a much wider range of theoritical influences. One of the most fundamental tenets is that we are unaware of many of our motives and that if these are known to us we are able to make better, less conflicted choices. However, we are often resistant to or defended against recognising these hidden motives termed unconscious by most psychodynamic theorists and hence are unable to change-indeed we seem to have a compulsion to repeat past behaviour. These repetitions are thought to arise because of earlier experience where our behaviour successfully enabled us to cope by ignoring or repressing difficult feelings. Psychodynamic counselling this has theory of why we are enabling to change, how this inutility arises and how it affects our lives.

Psycho-analysis is an intensive process, whereas psychoanalytic therapy is based upon psycho-analysis but is less intensive. Psychodynamic counselling evolve from psycho-analytic theory, however, it tends to focus on more immediate problems, be more practically based and shorter term than psycho-analytic theory. Goals of the psychoanalytic approach:

The goals of psycho-analytic approach are:

(i) To make the unconscious conscious;
(ii) To strive to probe into the deeper part of the psyche;
(iii) To get the issues those were not resolved during cognitive development;
(iv) To understand and experience the issues and to bring change in the character;

Principles of psycho-analytic theory: The general principles are:

(i) Help the person to tell his or her story.

(ii) Establish a solid working alliance.
(iii) Deal with resistance.
(iv) Gather background information and history.
(v) Select the problem or issue to be worked on explores the precipitating events.
(vi) Collaborate with the client to form a diagnosis and treatment plan.
(vii) Increase the client's awareness regarding defensiveness.
(viii) Revisit resistance to interventions.
(ix) Explore the client's transference.
(x) Examine how the past is impacting the present.
(xi) Help the client behave more effectively.
(xii) Provide feedback and confront discrepancies.
(xiii) Negotiate with the client regarding home work assignments.
(xiv) Remind the client of the termination date.
(xv) End therapy as agreed upon with the client.
(xvi) Schedule follows up as needed.

Conditions Influencing Counselling

The counselling process is influenced by several characteristics that help it become a productive time for the client and counsellor. Not all characteristics apply to all situations, but generally, the following help to bring about positive results.

(i) Structure
(ii) Setting
(iii) Client qualities
(iv) Counsellor's qualities

Physical setting: Counselling can happen any where, but the professional generally works in a place that provides:

(i) Privacy
(ii) Confidentiality
(iii) Quiet and
(iv) Certain comfort

When working with a client, you want to send a message that you are listening. This can be done by being attentive both verbally and non-verbally. The following Solar acronym will remind you about your physical setting which gives confidence to your client that you are listening.

S: Face the client squarely, that is, adopt a posture that indicates involvement.

O: Adopt an open posture sit with both feet on the ground to begin with your hands folded, one over the other.

L: As you face your client, lean toward him or her. Be aware of their space needs.

A: Maintain eye contact. Looking away or down seems that you are bored or ashamed of what the client is saying. Looking at the person suggests that you are interested and concerned.

R: As you incorporate these skills into your attending listening skills, relax.

Privacy Trust is an essential component in the development of helping relationships. Counselors regard the promise of confidentiality to be essential for the development of client trust. Most individuals seeking counselling services assume that what they divulge counselling will be kept in confidence by their counselor, with limited exceptions (Glosoff, Herlihy and Spence, 2000). This is most likely true for children and adolescents as well as adults. Managing confidentiality when counselling minors, however, is more complex than when counselling adults. School counselors must balance their ethical and legal responsibilities to their clients, clients' parents and school systems. This complex balancing act is one reason that the topic issues in school counselling. In attempting to weigh their legal and ethical obligations, it is helpful for school counselors to clearly identify those they consider to be clients. School counselors are part of an educational community. As such, they consult with teachers, administrators and parents. It is important for school counselors to clarify that their consultation is on behalf of students and that only the students are their clients (except if school counselors offer counsellingto students families).

The Code of Ethics and Standards of Practice of the *American CounsellingAssociation (ACA, 1995)* and the Ethical Standards for School Counselors of the American School Counselor Association (ASCA, 1998) are two resources available to help school counselors manage privacy and confidentiality in their counselling relationships. School counselors can also look to moral principles or shared beliefs or agreed upon assumptions that guide the ethical reasoning of helping professionals, (Remley and Herlihy, 2001, p. 3); upon which the codes of ethics are based. The moral principles most often cited in relation to ethical practices of counsellors include the following:

(i) Veracity or telling truth;
(ii) Justice or fairness;
(iii) Non-maleficence or doing no harm;
(iv) Beneficence or doing well;
(v) Autonomy or respecting free choice;
(vi) Fidelity or keeping promises.

The moral principle of beneficence refers to the responsibility to help clients gain something positive from engaging in counseling. It also includes counsellors' duty to – help society in general and people who are potential clients (Welfel, 2002, p. 34). Autonomy refers to respecting the freedom of clients to choose their own directions and make their own choices within the counsellingrelationship. Respecting a clients' autonomy does not mean that counselors encourage clients to make decisions independent of significant others (e.g., parents) in their lives or regardless of community and cultural implications. It does mean that – counsellors refrain from imposing goals, avoid being judgmental and are accepting of different values (Herlihy and Corey, 1996, p. 4). Applying moral principles to situations involved in respecting the rights of minor clients served in school settings is not always easy. To be effective advocates for their clients' rights, school counselors must have a good grasp of issues related to the following concepts: the legal status of minors and the legality and ethics of privacy, confidentiality, privileged communication, and informed consent. Each of these are reviewed along with relevant ethical standards and factors that complicate school counselors' ability to maintain a relationship based on student's confidence that they can speak freely and without fear of disclosure. Finally, implications for the practice of school counsellors are presented.

The Legal Status of Minors

The ACA (1995) Code of Ethics and Standards of Practice specifically references the term minor twice, both in relation to matters of consent. The Ethical Standards for School Counselors (ASCA, 1998) include standards specific to counselling minors throughout the entire document. Neither setoff ethical guidelines, however, defines the term minor. Typically, eighteen are considered the legal age of majority, unless otherwise designated. Minors, therefore, can legally be defined as those persons under the age of eighteen.

Amendment XXVI (1971) to the US Constitution established the right of eighteen-year-old citizens to vote and by extension has influenced the generally accepted age at which minors are extended other adult rights. For example, eighteen is cited in the *Family Educational Rights and Privacy Act* (FERPA), as the age at which the transfer of rights from parents to students occurs (FERPA, 1974). School counselors, therefore are faced with eighteen as the age at which their clients are legally assumed to be mature, to have full ownership and controlof their privacy rights. The legal concept of the age of majority has implications for minor clients' rights to make choices about entering into counsellingas well as their rights to privacy and confidentiality. Overall, although monor clients have — an ethical right to privacy and confidentiality in the counselling relationship... [the] privacy rights of minor legally being to their parents or guardians *(Remley and Herlihy,* 2001, p. 184).

Isaacs and Stone (1999) noted that the Supreme Court has upheld parents' legal right to make critical decisions about their children. (The term parents refer to all who function in the parental role and have the legal rights of parents.) Many people consider the decision to enter into counselling to be an example of a critical decision. Further, because counselling is considered to be a contractual relationship, minors cannot legally agree to be counseled on their own *(Remley and Herlihy,* p. 179). There are some exceptions to this. For example, many states have enacted laws allowing for individuals younger than eighteen to receive counselling or medical services without parental consent. Additionally, most states have laws that allow minors to be declared legally emancipated from their parents and a few states allow to be deemed a mature minor and capable of understanding the ramifications of counselling.

Record Keeping Counsellor's record keeping practices are increasingly governed by legislation. In some provinces, new Freedom of Information and Protection of Privacy legislation and Personal Health Information Acts have given counselors new guidelines about the way they keep records. The federal Youth Criminal Justice Act will also influence counselors' practices on record-keeping. For school counselors, legislation regarding the administration of public schools adds other imperatives. Some provinces have synthesised these various legislative requirements into policy statements that provide counselors with a guide for the management of their counselling records.

In schools, pupil records are typically held in three areas: the cumulative file in the main office; the young offender file if one exists held in a secure location by the principal and the counselling or special education files normally maintained by the counsellor and resource teacher. The cumulative file component includes things such as identification information, parent/guardian information, citizenship, school history, relevant health information, academic information on marks, attendance, awards and correspondence and legal documents. Some counselling information, such as results of psycho educational assessments that may inform programming decisions can also be included in this file. The counselling and special education files typically included additional such as: special education or resource information; clinician reports and meeting notes; referrals to other agencies; diagnostic testing results and reports from service providers outside of the school such as hospitals and treatment facilities. The *Youth Criminal Justice Act* component contains information about a young offender that may be used; to ensure compliance with a court order; to ensure the safety of staff, students and others; and to assist in the rehabilitation of the young offender. Most legislation is in agreement that there are certain conditions under which a person may be refused access to information in a file. They are: if disclosure might cause an invasion of the privacy of a third party; if disclosure could be detrimental to the education of the pupil; if disclosure could cause physical or emotional harm to someone; or if disclosure could interfere with an enactment or investigation.

Personal Health Information legislation. (Manitoba's for example), adds additional conditions under which access may be refused. These include: if disclosure may endanger the mental or physical health or safety of a person; if disclosure may reveal information about person who has not consented to disclosure; if disclosure could identify a third party who supplied the info in confidence under circumstances where confidence could be expected; or if the information was compiled for legal purposes. *The Youth Criminal Justice Act* demands that the offender's file must be kept separate from any other record or the young person; that on other person has access to the information except if authorised under the Act; and that the record be destroyed when the information is no longer required for the purpose for which it was disclosed.

In cases of divorced or separated parents, the *Divorce Act of Canada* states that, Unless the court orders otherwise, a spouse who is granted access to a child of the marriage has the right to make inquiries, and to be given information as to the health, education and welfare of the child. Provincial family law usually supports this notion as in *Manitoba's legislation,* for example, which states: Unless a court otherwise orders, the non-custodial parent retains the same right as the parent granted custody to receive school, medical, psychological, dental and other reports affecting the child. *(Family Maintenance Act Manitoba).* While the legislation described about is very similar from province to province, it is important to check on the specific wording of these kinds of acts in your own jurisdiction. Counsellors are often concerned about transferring information when a student transfers to a new school.

Generally, both the cumulative file and the counselling or special education file must go to the new school. A strategy that will help give counselors some sense of security is to retain the counselling records themselves, and place a notice in the cumulative file to the effect that counselling information exists on this student and may be obtained by contacting the counsellor directly. In this way, the records can go form professional to professional, and their security and privacy be ensured. Many schools have the parents or students, (if they are the age of majority) , sign a release from to allow the transfer of these records. Lawyer, Robert Solomon and Consultant, Dennis Lucas have each offered suggestion about effective record keeping.

These ideas include:

(i) Keeping all entries in chronological order;
(ii) Recording information while it's fresh;
(iii) Making any alterations with a straight line, dated and initialed;
(iv) Sticking to behaviors and concise description;
(v) Staying away from diagnosis and interpretation;
(vi) Limiting records only to directly relevant info;
(vii) Including record keeping information in your informed consent form, Record ingredients may include:
(viii) Name and date:
(ix) Presenting issue:
(x) Past history of issue (if described in an earlier record);
(xi) Current status of issue changes since last visit:
(xii) Treatment/goals/homework/actions;
(xiii) Check-back date/time;
(xiv) Referral info: To whom, where, when, what was said;
(xv) Administrative info: timetable, credits, etc.

To ensure the protection of your students and yourself, it is important to check your employer's policies on access to information, the CCA Standards of Practice on record keeping, and the privacy legislation in your province. If no workplace policy exists, it is critical that such a policy on record keeping be created. In some provinces, requests for information can be referred to the individual appointed as Privacy and Access Coordinator for your school hoard. This individual can, with input from you, decide to release the whole record, release parts of it, or deny access altogether. Parents then have the right of appeal to a provincial privacy *adjudicator* such as the provincial *ombudsman* in provinces where these procedures are not mandated, it is important to follow the CCA policy that school counselors should make every effort to ensure that there is a school-based procedure in place to adjudicate any requests from parents or guardians for access to counselling records. As a proactive step to avoid misunderstanding with students and parents, it is essential to have a good informed consent form in place. A consent form used in a school setting may say something like this: In all discussions between us you have a right to expect that anything we talk about will remain confidential. We will respect and guard your right to confidentially very carefully, but you need to know that are a few cases where are a few cases where that may not apply.

These are the situations where information may by share with someone else:

(i) If you ask me to speak with someone else for you or give them information you wish them to have;
(ii) If I feel that you or someone else may being danger or in need or protection;
(iii) If a court orders the release of information;
(iv) If required by law, as in cases of child abuse;
(v) To consult with another professional person in confidence to try to find solutions or answers for you.

Legal and Ethical Considerations in Counselling

Counselors like all professionals have ethical responsibilities and obligations. The principal rule supporting ethical obligations is that the counselor must act with full recognition of the importance of client's rights, the ethics of the profession. Counselling is not a value free or neutral activity (Grant 1992).

It is a profession based on values, which are orienting beliefs about what is good and how that good should be achieved.

(Bergin 1985) the relationship of moral standards and values, individual or cultural, in the life of that client.

Professional bodies of counselling have development ethical standards for which they have made available to the practitioners. Professional organisations for practicing counselling and psychotherapy are:

(i) American Psychological Association (APA);
(ii) British Association for Counselling (BAC), and;
(iii) American Counselling Association (ACA).

Need for ethical codes: Ethical codes help professionalise and protect an association by government and promote stability within the profession. The needs for ethical cods are:

(i) To control internal disagreement.
(ii) To protect practitioners from the public
(iii) To protect client from incompetent counsellors.

Especially in mal practice issues. Clients can also use codes to evaluate questionable treatment from the counselors. Ethical issues:

(i) Ethical codes are not set in stone. They serve as principles upon which to guide practice.
(ii) There are two dimensions to ethical decision-making:
(iii) Principle ethics: Overt ethical obligations that must be addressed.
(iv) Virtue ethics: Above and beyond the obligatory ethics and are idealistic.

Ethical Issues

(i) Ethical codes and standards of practice for counselors have been formulated by the American Counselling Association (ACA) and American Psychological Association (APA).
(ii) Ethical codes are guidelines for what counselors can and cannot do.
(iii) Each counselling situation is unique and sometimes the counselor must interpret the code.

Ethical Issues that influence Clinical Practice

(i) ***Client Welfare:*** Client needs come before counselor needs and the counselor needs to act in the clients' best interest.
(ii) Informed Consent Counselors need to inform clients as to the nature of counselling and answer questions so that the client can make an informed decision.

(iii) ***Confidentiality:*** Clients must be able to feel safe within the therapeutic relationship for counselling to be most effective. What the client says stays in the session unless the client is threatening harm to self or others.

Ethical Issues that influence Clinical Practice

(i) ***Dual Relationships:*** When a counselor has more than one relationship with a client (e.g. The counselor is a friend and the counsellor).

(ii) ***Sexual Relationships:*** Professional organizations strongly prohibit sexual relationships with clients and in some states it is a criminal offense.

Privileged Communication

(i) It is legal protection of the client which prevents a counselor from disclosing what was said within the counselling sessions(s).

(ii) This right belongs to the client and not counsellor.

(iii) Laws concerning privileged communication vary from state to state.

When to break confidentiality

(i) Tara off is Board of Regents of the University of California. A landmark case with the end result being that counselors have a – duty to warn if a client threatens another person's life or with significant bodily harm.

(ii) When a child under the age of eighteen is being sexually abused.

(iii) If the counselor determines the client needs hospitalisation.

(iv) If the information is involved in a court action.

Privileged Communication Doesn't Apply

(i) When a counsellor is performing a court ordered evaluation.

(ii) When the client is suicidal.

(iii) When the client uses the counsellor.

(iv) When the client uses a mental disorder as a legal defence.

(v) When an underage child is being abused.

(vi) When a client discloses intent to commit a crime or is dangerous to others.
(vii) When a client needs hospitalisation.

Legal Issues and Managed Care

(i) Counsellors have the duty to appeal adverse decisions regarding their client's.
(ii) Counsellors have a duty to disclose to clients regarding the limitations of managed care and the limits of confidentiality under managed care.
(iii) Counsellors have a duty to continue treatment and are not supposed to – abandon a client just because the client does not have the financial means to pay for services.

Malpractice

(i) When a counselor fails to provide reasonable care or skill that is generally provided by other professionals and it results in injury to the client.
(ii) Four conditions must exist.
(iii) The counselor has duty to client.
(iv) The duty of care was not met.
(v) The client was injured in the process.
(v) There was a close causal relationship between the counselor's failure to provide reasonable care and the clients injury.

Suggestions on Avoiding Malpractice Precounseling: Make sure to cover all information counselling:

(i) The financial costs of counselling.
(ii) Any special arrangements.
(iii) The competencies of the counsellor.
(iv) Avoid dual relationships.
(v) Clearly indicate if a treatment is experimental.
(vi) Identify limits confidentiality.
(vii) Help the client make an informed choice.

Suggestions on Avoiding Malpractice (continued) ongoing Counselling:

(i) Maintain confidentiality.
(ii) Seek consultation when necessary.
(iii) Maintain good client records.
(iv) Take proper action when a client poses a clear and imminent danger to themselves or others.
(v) Comply with the laws regarding child abuse and neglect.

Termination of Counselling:

(i) Be sensitive to the client's feelings regarding termination.
(ii) Initiate termination when the client is not benefiting from services.
(iii) Address the clients' post-terminations concerns.
(iv) Evaluate the efficacy of the counselling services.

An Ethical-Legal Decision-making Mode:

(i) Determine if an ethical-legal issue needs to be addressed.
(ii) Address contextual issues such as culture and personal bias.
(iii) Formulate an ethical-legal course of action.
(iv) Implement an action plan.

Counsellor Competence

(i) Counsellors need to accurately represent their credentials and qualifications.
(ii) Counsellors need to continue their education.
(iii) Counsellors need to only provide services for which they are qualified.
(iv) Counsellors need to keep up on current information of the field and especially in specialty areas.
(v) Counsellors need to seek counselling when they have personal issues.

Ethical and Legal concerns: Major areas related to ethical eight legal issues must focus on the following major areas:

(i) Informed consent,
(ii) Confidentiality,

(iii) Duty to warn/duty to protect.

Pertinent Legal and Ethical Issues

(i) Any appropriate course of action must be determined on a case by case basis.
(ii) Any policy requiring automatic dismissal or withdrawal of a student who expresses disturbing behaviour is legally vulnerable.
(iii) The issue is often about assessing risk.
(iv) A significant risk constitutes a high probability of substantial harm not just a slightly increased, or remote risk.
(v) Any assessment must be based on a reasonable *onedical* judgement relying on the most current medical knowledge and the best available objective evidence.

If you analyse all the legal & ethical issues concerned with counselling you can conclude it in the words of mark twain that to be good is noble, but to teach others to be good is nobler and less trouble. Governance of professional practice by Ethics and Law: Law is created by legislature and courts. It governs citizens of federal, country and state. Whereas ethics rooted in philosophy, crated by Professional associations like APA and ACA. It governs members of profession and guide practice. How can you consider an issue as legal or ethical? We can consider an issue as legal if:

(i) Lowers are involved,
(i) Matter has come to court,
(iii) The counsellor may be in danger of being accused of misconduct.

12

Career Information Counselling

Objectives

Career information, guidance and counselling refers to services that assist individuals, of any age and at any point throughout their lives, to make educational, training and occupational choices and to manage their careers. It includes services provided to those who have not yet entered the labour force, services to job seekers, and services to those who are employed. It includes a wide-range of activities. For example:

(i) Activities within schools to help students clarify career goals; understand the world of work and develop career-management skills;

(ii) Personal advice, guidance or counselling to assist with decisions about initial courses of study, courses of vocational training, further education and training, initial job choice, job change, or work-force re-entry;

(iii) The organised and systematic use of community members such as employers, alumni, parents and peers to provide occupational and educational advice and information; and

(iv) Print-based, computer-based or on-line services to produce and disseminate information about jobs and careers, courses of study and vocational training to help individuals make career choices.

Career information and guidance services have traditionally been seen as a public service available from educational institutions, government departments and their agencies. Increasingly, in countries competing in the global economy, common notions about career information and career development are emerging:

(i) It is an individual responsibility — services should help people help themselves manage their career development. This is career self-management;
(ii) It is an ongoing (life-long) learning process;
(iii) It is everybody's business and not just something undertaken at a time of crisis;
(iv) It requires worker and learner flexibility and adaptability, changes in the nature of work and employment require that most individuals be prepared to successfully manage several work and learning transitions; and,
(v) It requires different kinds of tools and services at different points across the life span.

In most countries, there are gaps and overlaps in the career information and guidance services. Availability is uneven. Few countries, it seems, have coherent policies, systems and delivery structures for career information and guidance that support transitions across the span of life, learning and work. Several challenges tend to be common across countries and provide an important context for considering local level services;

(i) Services to youth and adults have tended to be separate, thereby not reinforcing life-long access to learning, skill and career development;
(ii) Guidance and career development is both a specialised field and, at the same time, is part of many social services whose focus is not exclusively guidance. Social work, community development and rehabilitation are some examples. The issues of qualifications and assuring quality service are therefore complex;
(iii) Access to ongoing learning opportunities tends to be offered by employers who already have highly skilled work forces. This

learning/skill divide has significant economic and social implications;

(iv) There has been an explosion of technology, resulting in more resources devoted to developing career information systems and self-service delivery systems and at least the perception of fewer resources devoted to career counselling and guidance services than ever before;

(v) In many countries services for youth within the educational systems have often focussed on at risk and marginalised youth and/or on post-secondary bound youth. The school to work bound population has received less emphasis and there is risk they may fall through service cracks once.

(vi) In general, services to adults have been spotty. This is perhaps based on an employment model which is increasingly being questioned, in which adults, once attached to the labour force, were expected to remain attached with permanent and sustainable work and limited career change.

Strategies

Strategies that focus on a consolidation of services under one national government department or another may not necessarily result in the provision of coherent and seamless career information and guidance services across the life span. Many different kinds of support are likely needed from a variety of agencies. Support is needed where people learn, live and work. And it has to be relevant to their community context.

The *Organisation for Economic Cooperation and Development (OECD)* recognises that career information and guidance delivery strategies centered at the local (community) level are essential. There are many fine examples of local level co-operation and partnerships that respond to one or more of the challenges outlined earlier.

Well-organised career information, guidance and counselling services are important to education systems and to the labour market, as well as to their interface. Many arguments in support of this assertion are long-standing, but have been strengthened or refined by more recent developments within education systems and labour markets: both by trends in the ways that these are organised and operate; and by thinking within public-policy and other for how they might be organised and operate more effectively.

There are analogies between the importance that well-organised systems of information and advice play in improving the efficiency of education systems and labour markets, and the role that they play in improving the efficiency of financial or other markets. Ignorance is rarely bliss, and information about complex systems is often insufficient by itself. It needs careful organisation and can need sympathetic interpretation if it is to be of value in improving decision-making. Context and relevance, trust and shared understanding, each help to mediate information flows and information use.

Within education systems, career education has an important role to play within compulsory education in laying the foundations for life-long career development. These include knowledge and competences regarding self-awareness, the world of work, and making decisions and transitions.

Well-organised career information, guidance and counselling are particularly important in post compulsory education. Here, wider curriculum choice results in more diverse and complex routes into later stages of education, into employment, or into both. Where choices are more complex and their consequences are more costly, effective advice and guidance on educational options, and on links between these options and later occupational destinations, can help to better match individuals' learning choices to their interests, talents and intended destinations. This can help to:

(i) Reduce drop-outs from and back-tracking within education systems, and thus improve internal flows;
(ii) Improve flows between different levels of education, thus raising national levels of educational attainment; and improve transitions from education to the labour market.
(iii) These outcomes help to make better use of educational resources, and to increase both individual and social returns to investments in education.

Arguments within education systems for the importance of well-organised systems of career information, guidance and counselling receive greater prominence when national governments commit themselves to implementing policy frameworks that can make life-long learning for all a reality. This is because the notion of life-long learning stresses:

(i) The central role of individual learner demands in driving the learning that is provided, how it is provided and where and when it is provided.
(ii) Stronger links between education systems and the labour-market, and better systems for translating labour-market signals into educational choices.
(iii) Wider access to learning throughout all stages of life, often by those who have been away from formal learning for many years.
(iv) Wider access to learning by groups who are under-confident in, unskilled in, or unused to negotiating access to, complex learning systems. If such individuals are to have wider access to learning, many will need to have access to the information and advice required to make it possible.

Within the labour-market, well-organised career information, guidance and counselling can:

Improve the accuracy and accessibility of the information available to individuals about short and long-term job opportunities. In turn this can improve individual decision-making about jobs and about job training opportunities, and improve the allocation of human talents within the labour-market. In particular, well-organised career information, guidance and counselling can help to:

(i) Achieve a better match between skills, interests and qualifications on the one hand, and available job opportunities on the other; and
(ii) Unearth the talents of those who are not favoured by life's circumstances, thus improving the social and inter-generational mobility of talent.

(iii) Help to improve the allocation of labour across regions, industries and occupations in the face of labour supply, and demand fluctuations resulting from technological and structural change; and

(iv) Make a key difference between the successful and unsuccessful implementation of active labour-market programmes and active welfare-to-work programmes (together with other support services).

Roles of Information, Guidance and Counselling

These roles for information, guidance and counselling career services becomes increasingly relevant as human knowledge and skill come to play an increased role, compared to capital and labour, in national economic performance. They become still more important in the context of discussions about new concepts of careers that emphasise individual responsibility for career management, and individual and corporate responsibility for developing employability skills, often as a substitute for long-term commitment or loyalty.

Differences in institutions and traditions both constrain and provide opportunities in different countries. All countries face choices in the ways that career information, guidance and counselling services can be configured to meet key public goals such as life-long learning for all and active labour-market policies.

One way to elaborate upon these options is to develop "scenarios" or "models". These would incorporate a range of dimensions, and of options within each dimension. Possible dimensions for such scenarios, and examples of options within these, might include:

The role of the state

(i) Direct provider,
(ii) Main funder,
(iii) Residual funding source in areas of market failure;
(iv) Quality assurer,
(v) The role of the profession and other parties;
(vi) Professionally qualified staff acts as the principal provider of services.

(vii) Organisations representing professionally qualified staff acts as the principal standard setters and quality assurers.

(viii) Substantial service provision occurs through para-professionals such as information officers and subject teachers.

(ix) Substantial service delivery occurs through community members such as parents, employers, alumni and peers.

Governments directly pay for and provide virtually all services, with little contribution by individuals or enterprises. Nearly all service delivery staffs are employed by the *Central government organisations*. Governments pay for virtually all services, but provide very few directly, with most services being provided under contract by a wide range of decentralised agencies.

Governments pay for services to designated target groups – mostly youth, the disadvantaged and those on low incomes and individuals and enterprises pay for the bulk of other services.

Governments control quality through the qualifications that are required of the staff, who they employ to provide services and through the quality implicit in public delivery.

Voluntary standards, developed by professional associations of guidance workers, exist for staff skills/staff qualifications/service delivery/career information.

Government-developed or –endorsed standards exist for staff skills/staff qualifications/service delivery/career information and are used as a basis for resource allocation, recruitment decisions and the like.

Most career information is created and disseminated by governments. Governments contract out most of the production of career information, both print and electronic, to private publishers. A large number of private publishers compete to produce and sell print and electronic career information.

Government-funded organisations such as schools and employment services are funded to purchase information from their preferred private suppliers.

The production of "league tables" or guides that rank institutions allowing potential students to compare post-secondary educational institutions is common in the private market for career information and is encouraged by governments. Information on salaries, employment rates, vacancy rates and the like is standard in occupational information.

Educational and course information regularly includes information on student destinations, employment rates, earnings and the like. Most of the clients for career guidance services are students and public employment service clients.

Development of OECD

The field of career guidance contains a rich literature on theory and practice. In late 2000 the OECD's Education Committee and its Employment, Labour and Social Affairs Committee each endorsed a new activity on policies for career information, guidance and counselling services. This is a fairly new development for the OECD. In the mid—1990s the Centre for Educational Research and Innovation conducted case studies of national approaches to career guidance for youth, and pointed out that recognition of the importance of career guidance was only just beginning to move from the professional literature into the reality of policy.

A recent study has commented briefly upon the roles of personal advisers within welfare to work programmes and upon the tools that are required for them to do their jobs effectively.

However, in general the policy issues involved in the organisation, management and delivery of information, guidance and counselling services have not been treated comprehensively in OECD work.

Many individual examples of good practice, information and guidance systems are frequently not well- organised in many countries, and have often not been given a sufficient priority by those responsible for youth transition policies. Similar observations have emerged from a current OECD thematic review of adult learning. One purpose of the proposed new activity on information, guidance and counselling services is to follow-up these observations. The new activity has, however, wider purposes.

The OECD's current mandate from Education Ministers requires it to explore ways in which life-long learning for all can be made a reality. In its detailed elaboration, the notion of life-long learning for all involves more flexible pathways through initial education, easier re-entry mechanisms for adult learners, stronger links between initial education and training and the further education and training of adults, more flexible mechanisms for the recognition of knowledge and skills acquired outside of the classroom, and a more student-centred approach to learning that gives the individual greater control over the content, mode and location of learning.

In turn, all of these require, if they are to become a reality for larger numbers of learners, more effective "learning signposts" in the form of information guidance and counselling services.

Delivery of Information

This brings questions of the organisation and delivery of information, guidance and counselling services to the heart of a key public policy concern. At the same time, many countries have been adopting more active approaches to policies for the unemployed and for welfare recipients: the concept of mutual obligation is becoming more widespread, with the receipt of government income support often being contingent upon the individual developing an individual action plan, in association with a counsellor or adviser, to re-engage in active job search, education or training.

Taken together these developments in education policy, in labour-market policy and in welfare policy imply a greatly increased role for information, guidance and counselling services.

In short, how can the ways in which career guidance services are shaped to meet some key public policy objectives?

Twenty years ago, if faced with questions such as this, governments would have had few options. Like other personal services such as hair-dressing, career guidance had traditionally been delivered largely in a one-to-one, face-to-face mode that provided limited scope for productivity gains.

Twenty years ago governments, confronted with challenges such as those outlined above, would have been faced with a choice of either expanding access to services at substantially increased cost to the public purse, or of keeping costs manageable by setting tight criteria for access. Another option would have been to ration access by price, with major implications for equity and fairness.

However, over the last two decades, and in particular over the last decade, new techniques and new technologies have provided substantial scope for productivity gains in the delivery of career information and guidance services.

Developments in communications technology, including call centre technology, have opened up new possibilities for telephone information, advice and counselling services. Another way to increase the productivity of careers assistance services is to systematically involve others, who are not necessarily career professionals and to make use of their expertise and knowledge.

Examples include programmes to bring employers and parents into schools to talk about jobs and careers that they are familiar with, community mentoring programmes, careers fairs that involve many employers, industry associations and educational institutions, and the type of systematic use of alumni that is found in the careers services of Japanese colleges and universities.

All of these developments and approaches require career development professionals to learn new skills and to work in new ways. While these new options and new techniques might be seen by some as a way simply of reducing the cost to government of providing career information and guidance, a much more positive view is to see them as a way of greatly opening up access to career information and guidance without incurring a substantial increase in unit costs.

By themselves, they are not a solution to the questions that were posed above about how career information and guidance can assist to implement broad public policy objectives such as the implementation of life-long learning for all. But they must be an important part of the solution when put into the context of questions about access, quality, financing methods and the like.

The challenge is to draw a comprehensive picture of the organisation, delivery and staffing of career information, guidance and counselling services that includes them as one element in overall strategies to achieve goals such as life-long learning and active labour-market and welfare policies. Within the broad approach that has been outlined above, there are a number of specific issues and questions that will be examined in the new OECD activity on policies for career information and guidance that started late in 2000.

Occupational Information

Educational and occupational information that is used in information, guidance and counselling services: how it is produced and by who, how it is targetted to clients, and whether standards exist for it. This asks about the ways in which information, guidance and counselling services are funded; the ways in which costs are shared; and the financial resources devoted to information, guidance and counselling services.

An important feature of the activity is the way in which the OECD is working in close partnership with the career guidance profession and other bodies. The OECD assisted in the organisation of the March 2001 international symposium, hosted by the *Canadian Career Development Foundation,* and the *European Commission* and the OECD will co-operate in the commissioning of consultants' papers for the activity.

13

Integrated Career Information

Over the past decade, many countries have witnessed significant changes in the structure of work and learning. The globalisation of markets and the need to remain competitive have led business and industry to seek increased flexibility in their work forces. Workers are increasingly expecting to move back and forth between education/training and work. These shifting expectations are creating greater demand for career information, career coun selling and guidance services.

There is much diversity across countries with respect to how these services are organised at the national, provincial or regional and local levels, and what models best meet the need for periodic and life-long services. But at the local level, many individuals are closely connected to their communities, and these communities have unique local labour-markets and opportunity structures. A "one size fits all" information and guidance service would make no practical sense; local approaches and local information are essential.

Life-long learning sits squarely at the centre of public policy in most OECD countries. For example, successive governments in Canada, the United States and the UK have allocated significant public funds for research, policy development, program design and delivery that support continuous learning among youth and adults. For those countries at least, life-long learning is on the short list of priorities for 2001 – 2005. Policy makers have promoted life-long learning over the past two decades as an important route to secure individual and societal welfare. It is an issue around which governments at all levels, community-based organisations, learning institutions, enterprises and unions have coalesced. For business, it is not a social but an economic issue.

Life-long learning among employees is the key to maintaining currency of skills. Organisations must provide learning opportunities over the span of a career in order to retain and develop valuable people. Life-long learning becomes a reality when:

(i) Different kinds of education and training are inter-connected, transparent and accessible to the learner (primary, secondary, post-secondary education; class-room, work-place and web-based learning);
(ii) Life and work goals are both served across the life span;
(iii) Individuals, institutions, organisations all have a means to plan and support continuous learning;
(iv) Learning is clearly situated in a career development process; and,
(v) Learning opportunities are accessible for all workers.

The kinds of skills that form the human capital in a country range from job task specific ones to essential skills that are used both at work and in daily life. The skills needed in a growing knowledge economy change constantly. Clearly, skill development starts in elementary school and extends to people in their retirement years. Meeting skill needs involves all levels of government, public and private education, business, organised labour, the voluntary sector, and all sorts of community interest groups. For individuals, ongoing skill development is a key ingredient of career development.

Trends in Career Guidance Services

According to Watts, three major emerging trends appeared in the decade of the 1990s:

(i) Guidance is being viewed as a continuous process that should start early in schools, continue through the often extended transition period to adult and working life, and should then be accessible through out adult life;

(ii) A more open professional model is emerging as guidance specialists are expected to apply a range of interventions (e.g., curriculum programs, group work, computers and other media). They are more often working with and through networks of other individuals and agencies (e.g., supporting guidance roles of teachers and supervisors, and involving parents in the guidance process). The personal advisor role within the recent Connections program in England links guidance specialists more closely to front-line youth workers, and so is an application of a more open and networked professional model; and,

(iii) There is a greater emphasis on the individual as an active agent, rather than a passive recipient, within the guidance process.

There are also clear signs in several European countries of career information and guidance being accorded a higher priority than in the past. This is particularly evident in parts of the UK, especially in Scotland and Wales. Career information and guidance are seen as important measures in the improvement of people's skill levels, and in the full utilisation of a country's human resources. The delivery of career information and guidance services is also becoming deregulated.

In a few countries there has even been some limited application of market and/or quasi-market principles. For example, in the UK, many responsibilities of the Employment Eepartment for training and guidance have been devolved to Learning and Skills Councils (LSC's).

In France, the inter-institutional skills assessment centres (CIBC's) derive their income from assessments they carry out, with explicit costing and the threat of closure if they fail to attract clients.

In the Netherlands, more autonomy was given to schools to determine their own guidance structures within national guidelines. *The Advisory Offices on Education and Employment (AOB's)* offer services to schools, to the Manpower Service Organisation, and to employers on a contractual basis.

Decentralisation of service delivery has occurred to some extent in most countries. In Denmark, most initiatives are taken at the regional or local level. Just a few years ago in France, all guidance organisations were run by the central government. Now, a large number of initiatives and services are based on local structures or associations.

In Spain, Autonomous Communities have grown in importance, resulting in a diversification of guidance services. A complementary development is the formation of national councils that bring together a range of bodies directly involved, or with a stake in the delivery of career information and guidance services. Such national councils have been established in Denmark, The Netherlands, Italy and the UK.

In the United States, career information and guidance services are envisioned as an important component of the preparation of students for the world of work. Given its importance, the United States government has provided a legislative basis for federal support to career guidance and counselling in American schools. The first set of federal statutes is contained in the *Carl D. Perkins Vocational and Applied Technology Education Act of 1990.* The second is contained in the School-to-Work Opportunities Act (STWOA) of 1994.

Both the Perkins Act and STWOA call on state and local agencies to bring together partnerships of educators and businesses to build high quality school-to-work and vocational/technology education programs. Both laws call for professionally licensed and trained counsellors to administer career information and guidance programs. Another major trend in the US is the establishment of standards and professional and technical support in the delivery of career information and guidance services.

There are signs of an increasingly open and networked professional model seen in the certification of both professional Career Counsellors and Career Development Facilitators.

Leadership in this area, until 2000, was given by the *National Occupational and Information Coordinating Committee* (NOICC), and a network of parallel state committees *(SOICC's)*. This was a joint project of several US departments of government including Labour and Education. Career information, Information systems, and Career Development were together.

NOICC has now been replaced by the *American Career Resource Network* and *State Career Resource Networks*. In this current structure, there has been a separation between career developments which is within the Department of Education while information systems are within labour.

Privatisation and decentralisation have become *buzz* words for all levels of government and almost every government agency in Canada. The method of "outsourcing" and the providers of services may vary, but the result is the same. Fewer social services are being provided directly by government staff, with larger numbers of non-government agencies involved in the service delivery. Career information and guidance services are, in the main, public services, available through educational institutions, provincial and federal departments, and municipal agencies.

Career, employment and outplacement counselling in the private sector have existed for many years, largely on a fee for service basis for those able to pay. But the landscape has changed. Many more private practitioners are providing services under government contracts to a more diverse clientele. Service provision under these agreements continues to be free of charge for the clients.

The largest numbers of practitioners work under the umbrella of not-for-profit community groups. This is also an extremely diverse group with multiple skill sets and diverse professional backgrounds. Public policy in Canada over the past five years or more has emphasised individual responsibility and self-sufficiency or autonomy in career development. Youth and adults are encouraged to independently use the materials and services available through federal, provincial/territorial, or community-based resource or career centres.

All levels of government have poured the lion's share of funding into client self-service. Much of the impetus for self-service comes from government's desire to reduce the cost of services. It is also being driven by the rapid development of Internet technologies offering high levels of interactivity, visual appeal, and even the use of audio communications. Career information can be more efficiently delivered over the Internet in a self-service mode than can career guidance and counselling.

Cost-benefit research continues to be needed on the effectiveness of different delivery methods for different clients to provide a foundation for resource allocation.

14

Career Guidance: The Skills, Training and Qualifications

Objectives

Professional training, qualifications and skills were one of the five transversal issues recently discussed at the *Second International Symposium* on Connecting Career Development with Public Policy. While the focus at the Symposium was on the role of policy makers with respect to this issue, several separate observations on training, qualifications and skills were made.

These were:

(i) Training programmes have not kept pace with the changing career context which service recipients experience; they do not address the diverse career paths and complex labour-market that clients encounter.

(ii) There is little policy regarding the need for training programmes to prepare counsellors to effectively use internet resources.

(iii) Training related to helping guidance providers to be more effective in addressing accountability issues is mainly absent.

(iv) Advances in ICT and the concept of life-long learning appear to be the driving forces behind reforms of training in the very few instances where such reform in occurring.

(v) Regulation of entry to employment as guidance workers tends to apply to the education sector than to the labour-market sector. The private sector of careers services is unregulated in most countries.

(vi) There appears to be little linkage between training institutions and policy-makers.

(vii) Few countries have addressed the issue of diversity of qualifications versus the traditional professional qualification model.

A small number of international studies have examined issues relating to the skills, training and qualifications of guidance workers. A similar methodology was used in a comparative study of guidance services in higher education in the European Union.

Guidance services were classified by focus and level. Focus related to educational guidance, vocational guidance, and personal guidance. Level referred to first-in-line services (as part of the formal teaching function, e.g., learner support); second-in-line services (as for the first but with some degree of specialisation, e.g., study adviser/counsellor); and third-in-line services (separated from the formal teaching function, and offered by specialists, e.g., career/psychological counsellor).

There was much diversity in training, roles, and qualifications required, varying from little if any training for first-in-line to highly trained and qualified for third-in-line. Specialist career services were the fastest growth area of the guidance field in higher education across Europe. The issue of professionalism surfaced particularly for three groups—careers advisers, counsellors, and psycho-therapists—with boundaries being defined through their relationship to the discipline and profession of psychology.

The new/future skill needs of counsellors identified by European national correspondents were:

(i) Skills to respond to the increasing diversity in the student body, including diversity among EU students, i.e., multi-cultural and inter-cultural competencies in the broadest sense.

(ii) Skills in preparing clients to select and assess available information from ICT sources.

(iii) Skills to deal with increased numbers of students: Brief interviews, brief therapy.

(iv) A holistic approach in terms of guidance services to be provided to students. A study of educational and vocational guidance services in Europe, Educational and Vocational Guidance in the European Community, funded by the European Commission, examined inter alia the changing role of professional guidance services, including the training and qualifications of guidance workers.

Some associations of trainers and practitioners have set out what they consider to be good practice in the curriculum of the initial training of guidance workers. In the USA, for example, the Council for Accreditation of Counselling and Related Educational Programs (CACREP) has established national standards for such training. The Council's position is that all counsellors, regardless of their speciality, should experience curriculum in the area of human growth and development, social and cultural foundations, helping relationships, group work, career and lifestyle development, appraisal, research and program evaluation, and professional orientation.

In Europe, there is a *nascent* coming together of trainers of guidance workers through annual conferences that to date have centred more on the theory and practice of guidance than on training issues. The sixth European Conference of Guidance Trainers was held in Durham, UK, in 2000. The International Association for Educational and Vocational Guidance (IAEVG) is the main international forum for guidance practitioners and trainers. In a content indexing of all articles published in its Bulletin since 1979, only two articles directly focussed on counselor training, one addressing the European dimension in counselor training and the other discussing training counsellors for work in business and industry.

The IAEVG is currently undertaking a study of the competencies needed by guidance counsellors. The aim is to define a set of competencies required by educational guidance and career services providers in different countries with the aim of developing international qualification standards. Based on a literature review and feedback from the International Steering Committee for the study, a set of core competencies have been identified together with ten specialisations. The core competencies include:

(i) Ethical behaviour and professional conduct,
(ii) Advocacy and leadership,
(iii) Inter-cultural awareness,
(iv) Ability to apply theory and research to practice,
(v) Ability to communicate effectively,
(vi) Designing, implementing and evaluating guidance programmes,
(vii) Awareness of one's professional limitations,
(viii) Ability to use computers,
(ix) Ability to co-operate in a team of professionals,
(x) Knowledge of the life-long career development process.

Training of Guidance Practitioners in the Education Sector

Across countries and within the education sector the range of training varies considerably, from five years (France, Portugal) to several weeks (Denmark, Netherlands). The distinguishing feature here is the relationship to psychology and teaching. In France and Portugal the guidance worker possesses the equivalent of a basic degree in psychology plus a two-year post-graduate specialisation in vocational psychology.

In Denmark and the Netherlands the guidance worker is a teacher and has undertaken a short course in guidance. The commonality between those apparent extremes is guidance as learner support, requiring an expert knowledge of the principles of learning and teaching (educational psychology) and the application of this knowledge to educational and vocational decision-making and transitions (vocational psychology). The differences, apart from tradition, relate to the location of the guidance service and other roles that the guidance worker may be called upon to play.

In France the guidance worker is a staff member of the Centred' Information et Orientation. In Denmark the guidance worker is a staff member of the school and will also undertake subject-teaching duties. The type of training also influences the professional title of the guidance worker. In France the worker possesses the title of conseiller d'orientation psychologue; in Denmark the worker may possess the title of VET counselor or school and youth guidance educator.

Between the French and Danish examples lies a range of graduate and post-graduate qualifications. In Germany one may choose work science or social science in teacher education, enabling the possessor to provide career-related learning within the school system. In Spain guidance workers may combine first degrees in pedagogy, psycho-pedagogy or psychology with a further two-year specialisation in guidance. Guidance can be also a one-year post-graduate specialisation for persons possessing teaching qualifications in Ireland. The recruitment pool from which guidance workers in education can be drawn varies across countries.

In Slovenia guidance workers are recruited from backgrounds in psychology, pedagogy, social work, special pedagogy, and defectology. This can lead to inter-disciplinary enrichment in the guidance services provided. It can also lead to fragmentation of services to the client/consumer, as the focus of guidance and/or the priorities of guidance worker activities will reflect the particular training undertaken and not necessarily respond to client needs.

Very little guidance activity takes place in primary schools. Where it does occur, e.g., Austria, Czech Republic, Denmark, Slovenia, and Spain, it tends to occur at the upper end of primary school. Where primary school completion takes place at age 11/12, very little formal career-related learning or guidance takes place before transition to the next stage of schooling. Guidance workers in education are most likely to function as such in second-level/secondary school. Such provision in second-chance schools and for adult participants in education is relatively underdeveloped.

In the absence of guidance workers in such settings, tutors/teachers/trainers provide assistance-based on their own experience and without any formal guidance training. In tertiary/higher education, the wide variation of services across countries reflects the wide variation within countries, this reflecting the differing views of guidance within very independent educational institutions. Guidance within tertiary/higher education is provided in diverse mode, carried out by a range of expert and non-career expert guidance workers. This is often evident in separate student services for careers, placement, counselling, therapy and health, and tutorial/academic advising. The training and qualifications profile of guidance workers is not as cohesive as in second-level education.

Qualifications in guidance are requirements for employment in the education sector in most countries in primary and second-level schools but not to date in other education settings.

Training of Guidance Practitioners in the Labour-market Sector

Training for guidance workers in the labour-market sector across countries is generally organised differently from parallel training in the education sector. The duration of training ranges from five years (Finland, Portugal) to several weeks (e.g., Australia, China (Hong Kong), Netherlands). The longer duration of training is related to the professional qualification of psychologist (Finland, Portugal) or guidance counsellor diplomate (Germany). There is a very wide recruitment pool from which guidance workers are drawn. A guidance qualification or a qualification in educational or vocational psychology does not tend to be a requirement.

Training of short duration is given on-the-job, sometimes in an alternate model (e.g., France). Such training is obligatory in France in order for the worker to have the title of conseiller a l'emploi. Additional and/more focussed training is often provided, e.g., in Ireland, to personnel working with specific target groups e.g., long-term unemployed, or youth at risk of social exclusion.

Training courses of short duration tend to be job-task-focussed and non-accredited. The private sector of guidance services is unregulated in most countries in terms of training and qualifications requirements.

Within both education and labour-market sectors across countries can be found a range of occupations and roles which support guidance workers in achieving the programme objectives of guidance services. Examples of these are Youth Information Officer (Ireland, Romania), Information Officer (in tertiary/higher education), and Librarian. While many may possess training and qualifications related to information science and/or communications, their support role in the guidance service is learned on the job and without any foundation in educational or vocational psychology.

Given the information explosion arising from the Internet, it is likely that such persons will increasingly play a key role in mediating information for guidance support purposes. Additional and complementary training in educational and vocational psychology and other disciplines will greatly enhance the roles they currently play in the guidance services.

There appears to have been very little systems change in the training and qualifications provided to and required of guidance workers in the past decade, whatever the changes in the content of the training. However, a number of new training programmes have been developed that support a more open professional model of guidance.

The examples below have been piloted through European Union Programmes and Initiatives, and their longer-term impact remains to be seen. Community-based Guidance Assistance:

(i) Significant adults and peers in disadvantaged communities and linked professionals, e.g., social and youth workers, have been trained in front-line guidance skills in order to provide guidance to "hard to reach" young people.

Adult Guidance

(i) **Training of Trainers:** Managers of adult education learning opportunities have been trained to establish, maintain market and quality-assure adult educational guidance services.
(ii) **Training Youth Reach Staff in Front-line Guidance Skills:** Trainers and tutors working with challenging young people in second-chance schools have been trained in basic guidance skills to enable them to work more effectively with such young people. In these pilot projects, training programmes attracted university accreditation in some countries.

The numbers of guidance workers that are being trained nationally appears to be mainly a function of the duration of training but not entirely so. Estimates provided show Denmark topping the league within the countries responding, with 1,000 personnel completing initial training annually. This compares with fifty guidance graduates reported for Germany. In the UK, around 370 persons complete initial training annually; however, there has been a major drop in the past three years in applications and registration for initial training and employers are reporting inability to fill vacancies.

The temporary solution used by UK careers services is to recruit unqualified staff and train them internally. This was regarded by all employers as an unsatisfactory solution, as it brought pressure on other staff, on financial resources, and on the quality of the service available to clients. No comparative studies similar to the UK have been undertaken in other countries. Indeed, national statistics of patterns of training applications, registrations, job applications, recruitment and retention of guidance workers are very difficult to come by.

This should be an issue of major concern to policy-makers in national human resource planning for guidance services in all sectors of the economy. The most significant difference within countries lies in the degree of prescription of qualifications for employment as a guidance worker in the education and labour market sectors.

There is tight regulation in qualification requirements for guidance workers in the education sector, particularly in primary and second-level schools. Tertiary/higher education is much less prescriptive in both careers and academic advising, with guidance training and qualifications requirements varying from none to post-graduate.

Adult educational guidance and guidance in second-chance schools have traditionally been provided by tutors/trainers without any formal guidance training, though this picture is now beginning to change. By contrast there are no guidance training and qualification requirements as pre-entry conditions for employment as a guidance worker in the labour-market sector. The wide gap between training and qualification requirements for guidance workers has other potential negative impact. Communication between education and labour-market guidance services may suffer, as both speak a different guidance language. Mutual negative perceptions increase.

Both can feel threatened by the others' professional standing. Above all there is little or no occupational mobility for guidance workers between the sectors. Where such flow is possible through recognition of guidance qualifications (e.g., Czech Republic, Ireland, Korea, Luxembourg, Norway, Romania, UK), it tends to be from the education sector to the labour-market sector. In many countries there is no mutual recognition of guidance qualifications between the education and labour-market sectors. Such recognition and consequent mobility would greatly enhance the development of a seamless guidance provision for clients.

The mobility issue referred to above is further compounded by lack of training and qualifications structures that would enable guidance workers to move from non-professional to professional status. In only two countries in Europe, Ireland (labour-market) and UK, is such movement possible at present. Structures facilitate movement from the equivalent of a two-year national certificate to under-graduate or post-graduate diploma levels.

The initiative for developments of this kind has been government-led (UK) or organisation-led. It is significant that progression for guidance workers from non-professional to professional status is a non-issue for trainers and professional associations in many countries. The absence of such progression pathways is a major source of frustration to guidance workers whose training has consisted of short non-accredited programmes and to other personnel who have had many years of experience in guidance roles without any training.

Across countries there is wide variation on who decides the content and methodology of initial training for guidance workers:

By trainers alone: Australia, China (Hong Kong), Finland, Netherlands, Spain, and Slovenia.

By the government ministry alone: France,

By trainers and the professional association together: Ireland (Education), Norway,

By trainers and the government ministry together: Austria, Czech Republic, Greece (Education), Luxembourg, Portugal, Romania.

By trainers, professional association and the government ministry together: Belgium, Finland, Denmark, Germany, Ireland (Labour), and UK.

By trainers and local authorities: Italy.

Nine approaches may be used individually or in combination for devising the content and methodology of initial training for guidance workers. These are:

(i) Formal job analysis;
(ii) Formal job review of guidance workers;
(iii) Review of guidance training nationally;
(iv) Review of guidance training internationally;
(v) Suggestions or prescription by the professional association;
(vi) Suggestions or prescription by government ministry;
(vii) Reaction to public demand;
(viii) Reaction by trainers to developments in the field of guidance;
(ix) Reaction by trainers to economic, social and information society developments.

Reactions by trainers, suggestion of government ministries and of professional associations appear to be the main source of shaping and developing the content and method of guidance training. Austria and Finland each combine all nine methods.

Germany and Spain use all except suggestions by the professional association and reaction to public demand. Denmark, on the other hand, depends entirely on reactions by the trainers to developments in the field of guidance and to economic, social and information society developments.

In overall terms, trainers play a key role in guidance curriculum development. Trainers themselves, however, are not very well-organised. There are no national or international associations of trainers of guidance workers. Trainer membership of national and international associations of guidance workers provides a proxy forum.

Cost of Training

The role of the government ministry is somewhat paradoxical across countries. In the six countries where decisions are left entirely to the trainers, funding is provided by the relevant government ministry (or ministries) with apparently no other input.

In France the relevant government ministry decides on content and delivery of training and funds it entirely. The approximate level of government funding support for the initial training of guidance workers is high, with 100 per cent in Finland, France, Germany, Luxembourg, Netherlands, and Norway.

Some governments support a number of student places e.g., Ireland (education), UK, in addition to providing general funding for higher education. Self-funding by participants is a strong dimension of funding of training in China, Denmark, Ireland (education), Slovenia, Spain and UK. Training programmes are often run on a shoe-string budget by training institutions. EU Programmes and Initiatives are currently a significant source of funding for training programmes in Greece.

Recurrent Training

Recurrent training is provided annually to guidance workers in most countries and participation in general is optional. The participation rate estimates vary from 100 per cent to ten per cent or less (France, Germany, and Luxembourg). Where participation is mandatory (e.g., Finland (Labour), Ireland (Labour), Portugal (Labour), the relevant government ministry funds the training.

Where such training is an option, it is also mainly funded by government and sometimes partly by the trainees and employers (Netherlands). In Argentina recurrent training is funded by guidance workers themselves. Incentives for participation range from salary improvement (Slovenia) to penalty for non-attendance (Finland). In most cases, reward for participation is either accreditation of training (e.g., Netherlands, Romania) or higher grade of membership of the professional association.

ICT and Distance Education

Very little use is made of ICT and Distance Education to deliver initial and/or recurrent training for guidance workers. ICT has been used for initial and recurrent training of guidance workers in Europe. The positive features cited for the use of ICT for training guidance workers are flexibility in terms of time and place of training, cost-efficiency, and uniformity of delivery.

In Greece, ICT and Distance Education are viewed as a means of increasing the number of training places for guidance workers. The limiting factors cited are that such approaches are not appropriate for group and interpersonal processes (Austria), and do not provide optimal conditions for behaviour shaping (Germany).

Other limiting factors cited are lack of investment (UK), access and hardware problems (Ireland (Labour), Romania), and lack of expertise and experience among trainers to deliver this training approach (Greece). There is a general preference for the traditional model of training involving face-to-face meetings for the purposes of sharing and exchanging ideas and experiences and for networking.

It is clear that the use of ICT and Distance Education for training guidance workers is not a priority or even on the agenda of trainers, professional associations and government ministries in many European countries. Progress in this field requires the commitment of these key actors. Such commitment is currently lacking. The lack of interest of European countries in developing this training modality contrasts with the USA where the Association for Counsellor Education and Supervision developed and adopted guidelines for online instruction in counselor education.

There appears to be a general unwillingness to examine the potential and experience of ICT and Distance Education for interpersonal and group processes or even to research such processes. The use of older media such as telephone and television for guidance delivery is also unlikely to appear in existing initial training programmes. It is as if training is time-bound by what is currently known about face-to-face inter-personal and group processes, with no thought being given to the psychological and social phenomena of non-face-to-face interaction. Given the apparent lack of recognition of such life and technological phenomena in guidance training in Europe, one could postulate a knock-on effect on how guidance training programmes treat the issue of ICT in delivery of careers information and guidance. There has certainly to be some modelling effect, positive and/or negative.

Countries such as Denmark, France, Germany, Ireland and Netherlands report that much importance is attached in their initial or recurrent training programmes to the use of ICT to deliver careers information and guidance. As to the preparation of guidance workers to work with and through non-professionals and the voluntary sector, only two countries, Ireland (adult educational guidance and labour-market services) and Greece, cited this as a key aspect in training for guidance workers. In many countries, e.g., Argentina, Czech Republic, Netherlands, Norway, Portugal, Romania, Slovenia and Spain, there appears to be a blind spot on this issue.

The increasing globalisation and internationalisation of education and employment receives more attention in guidance training in Austria, China (Hong-Kong), Denmark, Germany, Netherlands and Norway. It does not feature in training programmes for guidance workers in Belgium Portugal and Slovenia.

ICT is a significant methodology for delivering career information and guidance. Its applications and potential have been well-documented elsewhere. It does not yet appear to be attracting a significant time slot in guidance training in many countries. This can partly be explained by resistance to change in traditional methods of guidance, partly by lack of investment in providing the necessary hardware, software and internet connectivity by training institutions and government, and partly by a lack of good models of practice within countries of how the potential of ICT can be harnessed to deliver careers information and guidance.

Guidance is much more than a Face-to-Face Interview

SCAGES *(Standing Conference of Associations for Guidance in Educational Settings, UK)* identified eleven important activities of guidance:

(i) Informing
(ii) Advising
(iii) Assessing
(iv) Teaching
(v) Enabling
(vi) Advocating
(vii) Networking
(viii) Feeding back
(ix) Managing
(x) Innovation/Systems change
(xi) Signposting
(xii) Mentoring
(xiii) Sampling work experience or learning tasters
(xiv) Following up.

As indicated below, only some of these fourteen activities are covered in present quality guidelines or standards: in most cases, the main focus is on Informing and Assessing. Even the more comprehensive quality frameworks, for example the British Guidance Council Quality Standards, do not cover the full range of guidance activities. This leads to the reflection that—

(i)4 There is room for enhancing the coverage of quality issues in terms of activity areas in guidance.
(ii) Some issues/areas are relevant for particular guidance services: Few services would cover all fifteen areas.
(iii) Some issues/areas are left out of scope because they are seen as irrelevant, and/or difficult to measure, and/or politically sensitive.

In some countries, quality standards in career guidance build on staff performance or skills/competencies indicators, which are generally quite exhaustive. They comprise, e.g., advocacy, publicity, feedback, and quality assurance procedures.

Educational and Occupational Quality

One of the areas of careers guidance in which introducing quality standards is less complicated, yet still quite comprehensive is the informational side, which in many cases is pre-dominant in guidance provision. For example, the American NCDA quality guidelines in this area are highly detailed and cover most aspects related to career information services. Several sets of guidelines have been issued by the *NCDA*, including:

(i) Guidelines for the Preparation and Evaluation of Career and Occupational Information Literature;
(ii) Guidelines for the Use of the Internet for Provision of Career Information and Planning Services;
(iii) Guidelines for the Preparation and Evaluation of Video.

Career Media - Career Software Review Guidelines

The first of these sets of guidelines acts as a model for the others to some extent. It contains, among its general guidelines, a list of items to help editors of career information: Dating and Revisions, Credits, Accuracy of Information, Format, Vocabulary, Use of Information, Bias and Stereo-typing, and Graphics, followed by comprehensive Content Guidelines, all of which contribute to general good editorial performance. Other American standards, focussed on web-based career guidance, include standards issued by the *National Board for Certified Counsellors and*, focusing more on the informational side, standards issued by the Association for Computer-Based Systems for Career Information.

Denmark has issued a Declaration of Career Information (with a focus on information on training/educational options), i.e., a list of headings to be covered in all types of career information, regardless of the chosen media:

(i) Identification (who is imparting what to whom);
(ii) Goal (aims, target group, usage);
(iii) Contents (theme, coverage, style);
(iv) Medium (availability in different formats: hard copy, computerised);
(v) Structure (organised sequentially or as hyper-text);
(vi) Accessibility (computer specification; audio version of printed or computerised material).

The scope for umbrella organisations, governmental and NGOs alike, to issue guidelines on career information, is evident. It provides a relatively easy and cheap area in which to issue quality guidelines. Applying such standards or guidelines, however, is far more difficult, especially in the present versatile and volatile media environment. Standards or guidelines on career information, for good reasons, deal with the tip of the information iceberg, i.e., material produced and designed as career information.

No guidelines address the more clandestine type of information which is imparted every day in, e.g., TV series, sitcoms, documentaries, web-sites, and email-based guidance, in which a multitude of role models are depicted along with more or less biased and distorted information. Thus, the informational aspect of sustaining quality in career guidance and information, which looks relatively simple at first sight, and which is already promoted in some countries by clear guidelines, in fact turns out to be complicated and controversial. And probably impossible to implement in relation to modern integrated media.

Qualifications and Competencies of Staff

In an attempt to secure the overall quality of career guidance, the German Association of Career Counsellors maintains a Directory of Certified Career Counsellors. This directory is seen as important to secure transparency to clients of the formal competencies of guidance practitioners. The Institute of Career Guidance in the UK also now maintains a Register of Guidance Practitioners. This sort of strategic move is paralleled in other, more commercialised guidance cultures, e.g., in the USA where licensing forms a significant part of the path to professionalisation: licensure is an important feature in 44 states.

These regulations are linked with the quality assurance program offered by *CACREP (Council for Accreditation of Counselling and Related Educational Programs)*, whereby the quality of the training and education of professional careers guidance staff is regulated and maintained. This includes a lengthy quality assurance process: direct inspection of the premises, the curriculum, staff qualifications, etc.

People working in career development practice need to demonstrate certain attitudes. They need to be:

(i) Insightful,
(ii) Honest,
(iii) Open-minded, and
(iv) Results-oriented.

People working in career development practice need to have certain skills. They need to:

(i) Document client interactions and progress,
(ii) Accommodate diversity,
(iii) Collect, analyse and use information,
(iv) Convey information clearly when speaking and writing.

People working in career development practice need to have certain knowledge. They need to know:

(i) Career development models and theories,
(ii) The change process, transition stages, and career cycles,
(iii) Components of the career planning process,
(iv) The major organisations and resources for career,

Development and Community Services

All competency areas are important in providing comprehensive career development services. Currently, six main areas of specialisation have been identified:

(i) Assessment,
(ii) Facilitated Individual and Group Learning,
(iii) Career Counselling,
(iv) Information and Resource Management,
(v) Work Development,
(vi) CommunDity Capacity Building.

All career development practitioners will need to have a certain number of basic competencies in all six areas of specialisation.

Quality issues in guidance are often linked with other (related) phenomena. One of the links, in recent years, has been a growing interest in the relationship between the social and economic goals of guidance: the effects and effectiveness of guidance have been studied, along with cost-benefit ratios. Few evaluations have considered, specifically, the quality of economic outcomes of guidance itself, although implicit assumptions on the effects and effectiveness of different measures have been made.

One of the difficulties of measuring economic outcomes of guidance is the obvious one that it is very difficult to establish control groups, which are not affected by specific interventions.

First of all, it would be morally questionable to deprive certain groups of services which were given to everybody else; and secondly, guidance is difficult to *disentangle* from other forms of information and inspiration, from the influence of peer advice, the media, and chance, and from other elements of schemes of which they are an integral part.

Potentially, guidance offers benefits to individuals, education and training providers, employers, and governments. Guidance can play a role in fostering efficiency in the allocation of human resources, and social equity in access to educational and vocational opportunities. This is some of the policy rationale behind guidance provision in general. In economic terms, guidance can assist the operation of the labour market in three main ways:

(i) By supporting individual decisions (labour supply decisions, human capital decisions, and job search decisions)
(ii) By reducing labour market failures (drop-outs from training, mismatch, discouraged workers)
(iii) By contributing to institutional reforms designed to improve the functioning of the labour-market (open learning, job-and training rotation schemes, etc.).

Internationally, some research projects on the economic aspects of guidance have been carried out. But most have experienced considerable methodological difficulties:

(i) The effects of guidance are not likely to be visible for some time.
(ii) The longer the time that elapses, the more factors other than guidance come into play.
(iii) Controlled trials are the surest method of distinguishing effects from mere consequences. But such trials are difficult to mount, and more so over longer periods: control cannot be indefinitely extended, nor guidance indefinitely denied.
(iv) If the purpose of guidance is to help individuals to clarify and implement their own goals, this makes it difficult to find appropriate standardised criteria against which to evaluate the outcomes.

In short, it is a field with many pitfalls, as OECD has acknowledged. Moreover, the economic value of guidance as such, especially in integrated approaches (educationally-based guidance, for instance), is difficult to *disentangle* from other activities and interventions. On the other hand, guidance is clearly in a number of respects part of an overall attempt to create and obtain benefit from economic growth, the assumption being that economic growth will create more jobs. In this context, guidance is regarded as a cost-effective measure to curb unemployment, which in turn is seen as a waste of human and economic resources.

The economic rationale for a number of specific guidance activities is that they may shorten the periods of unemployment, create greater flexibility in the labour-market, or support mobility. In these broad terms, the quality of guidance is linked with its role as a market-economy facilitator, with a supposed economic impact, even if this is seldom in fact measured and documented.

With accountability, being moved up the agenda in most parts of the public sector, guidance in some EU countries, especially in the UK and the Netherlands, is measured with an economic yardstick: how much does guidance cost, and does it pay? One step further into this concept, guidance itself is put on the market, either through privatisation, or via guidance vouchers, as was the case in the UK as an experiment.

In these terms, a market in guidance itself is created, where ultimately non-profitable parts of guidance could be discarded at the expense of more vulnerable users, thus excluding the long-term unemployed and other vulnerable groups, whereas employed individuals would be able to pay for an extended service. In other guidance cultures, such market-oriented developments are not encouraged, or, indeed, seen as signs of quality in guidance.

Historically, there has been a profound interest in many 'developed' countries in measuring guidance, but from different perspectives. During the first half of the 1900s, the interest was linked with the prevailing psychometric testing tradition, where measurement was the very essence of guidance.

Interestingly, this tradition was abandoned in some countries, e.g., Denmark, for a number of reasons, both technical ones, and political ones.

In recent years, evaluations of the public sector have been numerous in many countries, especially in terms of quality assurance exercises. Thus, in terms of guidance, a study on the quality of Danish career guidance, listed a number of generic quality indicators:

(i) Client-centeredness,
(ii) Accessibility, transparency and coherence of the services,

(iii) Well-trained guidance staff,
(iv) Valid, precise and comprehensive careers information,
(v) Referral to other guidance specialists, and
(vi) Follow-up.

In Europe, one of the purposes of the Single European Market is to increase personal mobility within the European Union.

Career guidance may facilitate such mobility: Guidance is part of the globalisation process. The boundary less career is emerging, both physically and metaphorically. Mobility, however, is a coin with two sides: it may improve the quality of life for the mobile, but the processes of mobility tend to leave the immobile behind in poorer conditions.

The negative effects of mobility can include segmentation, segregation and marginalisation. In such manpower exporting areas, the loss of dynamic individuals may add to the cultural and economic downward spiral. In this picture, the role of career development becomes abundantly clear: career guidance/counselling is a vehicle for economic growth, the irony being that much of the growth is what has been labelled 'job-less growth'. In this capacity, one of its aims is to facilitate personal mobility, i.e., ease the movement of manpower (and students) to economic growth areas, thus serving as a societal lubricant.

Economic growth, in terms of career development, may be sustained by scientifically placing people in their proper occupational position: a testing tradition. Historically, in a reaction to the sometimes rather crude and mechanistic methods of psychometric testing, the client was moved to the centre of career guidance in what became known as the 'client-centred' approach: each individual has a potential of personal growth.

The guidance practitioner, in this perspective, is seen as a helper in the process of the individual's self-exploration.

In terms of economic growth, career counselling helps each individual to unfold his/her potential, thus providing a link between personal growth and economic growth. It follows from this brief historic outline that quality issues differ over time, according to the prevailing professional discourse and the societal circumstances.

Applying market-economy principles to careers guidance and information services implies that guidance either acts as a market facilitator (e.g., by helping to balance demand and supply in the labour-market), and/or is a market in itself (e.g., by selling career development services at a market price). The counsellor acts as a human capital investment adviser. But the analysis of cost-benefit ratios falls far behind a number of important issues, e.g., care for the underprivileged or environmental concern.

Nonetheless, the *International Association of Educational and Vocational Guidance (IAEVG)*, for example, have adopted a statement on global Ethical Standards, which focus on important humanistic values, and which include a recognition of the tensions between economic growth and environmental issues. In short, new concepts are under way to challenge or supplement the paradigm of economic growth as the basic parameter. The next section depicts some examples of such alternative quality concepts.

Other forms of measuring output and services (including, potentially, career guidance services) could serve as a corrective to the purely economic angle. Thus, Ethical Accounting, a method of describing values, goals and achievements which is used in some companies and educational institutions, could be an additional method in future for measuring the outcomes of career guidance.

The economic yardstick is one-dimensional; guidance and counselling are multi-dimensional interventions and need to include ethical considerations.

15

Placement and Follow-up Services

Placement

Placement is an important service in any guidance programme. Without placement, a guidance programme is incomplete because until and unless an incumbent is placed in a good job where he can utilise his maximum abilities and skills, and a continuous evaluation of his progress is made, the services are meaningless.

Placement refers to "assigning of a worker to the job for which he is judged best fitted". The term 'fitted' means the individual's satisfaction as well as his abilities in relation to the job. There are two types of placement services: (A) Educational placement and (B) Vocational placement. We will describe them in the following pages.

Functions of Placement Services

(a) ***Determining needs revealed by drop-outs and follow-up studies:*** In our country, the largest number of drop-outs is at the higher secondary school stage. The reasons of drop-outs may be many. How can the school prevent the high percentage of drop-outs? This question can be answered by placement workers who may gather information from drop-outs as regards their problems and also evaluate the total school programmes to minimize the percentage of drop-outs.

(b) ***Counselling of former pupils*:** Pupils, who dropped out return to the school in future for guidance. The counsellor can aid such dropouts by suggesting those courses which can help them in bringing efficiency in their work.

(c) ***Curriculum planning:*** Placement services help in planning, modifying and reconstructing the curriculum in the light of the data collected from the field.

(d) ***Occupational information:*** Placement personnel may collect information on problems peculiar to various jobs. They can provide useful information to the teacher of the occupations, on job getting technique, and trends in occupations.

Phases of Placement Services

(a) ***In the first phase*:** the general character of educational or occupational life is explained to the student and he received necessary education pertaining to Occupational life.

(b) ***In the second phase:*** the student is oriented to some educational or occupational field in which he is interested and about which he has sufficient educational experience.

(c) ***In the third phase*:** the student is enabled to understand his own interests and aptitude and to relate them to the educational or occupational areas under his study.

(d) ***The fourth phase:*** of placement service deals with the actual choice of an educational course or an occupation. It is the most important phase of placement service. The individual needs skilful guidance and counselling in choosing a job for himself. This is the stage when the guidance worker thoroughly evaluates the personality characteristics of the individual.

(d) ***In the fifth phase*:** the individual takes up the job and begins to perform actual duties.

(f) ***The last phase:*** of the placement service is follow-up of the job course provided to the individual.

Types of Placement Services

(A) **Educational Placement:** Educational placement consists of helping students' select appropriate curriculum, the subjects within a special class for gifted and slow learners and the like. Traditionally the curriculum followed needed upto 8th class in our country is uniform. Educational guidance is needed in class IX to select a suitable course out of the five groups in Arts, Science, Commerce, Agriculture and Technical Education.

The new pattern of education (10 + 2) recently accepted in the country provides a uniform curriculum upto 10th class and after 10th class, different streams are provided for the students.

Placement within a curriculum after the 8th or 10th grade level is extremely important because of its eventual influence on future career of the pupils.

Educational placement within school is concerned with placing students in school activities that will add to their development as individuals.

Placement helps the youth to meet their needs for social development, civic participation and personal growth. It helps in their selection of activities that contribute to their development in line with their interests and help them engage in more or in fewer activities as warranted. Educational placement may help pupils select the special courses that are suitable to them.

Some Characteristics of Educational Placement

Educational placement involves assisting pupils to obtain information in relation to higher educational and training opportunities.

It is the process of assisting the individual to reach the next step in the sequence of educational or training experiences which he accepts as appropriate for himself. It is more comprehensive than job placement. Following are the major characteristics of educational placement.

(a) *Educational placement affects all pupils:* Educational placement is a continuous process which aids all pupils to adjust to the new grades and the next school. The teachers and the administrators are concerned with adjustment of pupils in their present grade and school and also to prepare them for the next school. The personal information which teachers gather and record about each pupil accompanies him to the next grade and school in order to facilitate his adjustment by understanding his interests, aptitudes and academic achievements etc.

(b) *Articulation between schools palacement*: Assisting the individual to progress from one school to the next is a placement function For discharging this function successfully, the cooperation of the sending and the receiving school is essential The teachers should make clear to the individual with the opportunities open to him for further education and training. This function of placement services needs active cooperation between the schools.

(c) *Placement in training situations:* In our country, pupils may be divided into three categories (a) those who pass Higher Secondary or Intermediate and enter college, (b) those who pass Higher Secondary or Intermediate examination and seek employment, (c) those who drop out of school to work or to seek employment.

Some pupils will seek assistance to get admission to some technical or professional institutions while some others may need on-the-job training, etc.

The services involved in the placement process should be concerned with providing information, counselling and placement in accordance with the needs and interest of individual pupils.

(d) *Placement in co-curricular and community activities:* Some of the educational opportunities which may serve pupils are found outside the school's instructional programme and others exist beyond the four walls of the school. Certainly, the co-curricular activities offer opportunities for exploring pupils' interests and aptitudes. Likewise many community activities offer developmental experiences for pupils. It is the responsibility of the school to identify co-curricular activities in the school and the community which offer desirable experiences for pupils. Once these activities have been explored, the school needs to recognize the functions of placement. Aiding pupils to utilize those who promise to serve the needs and interests of individual is the responsibility of the placement worker.

The school should help pupils to relate their interests to co-curricular opportunities and to see that those activities which serve their needs and interests are made easily available to them.

B. Vocational Placement

Vocational placement includes assisting the youth to secure part time and full time employment after their school career is over and placement in post-high school education and training situations. The university educational guidance and vocational guidance department (A list of universities which have department and bureaus of vocational guidance is appended at the end of this book) can play an important role in providing information on the labour market at local, state and national levels. But types of services which are provided at present in the university bureaus to the vast majority of students are not of great use because the bureaus have no separate accommodation, meagre resources and one or two members of staff who are not duly qualified to provide guidance services in the universities.

Some Characteristics of the Job Placement Service

Effective job placement services are an essential part of the total guidance services. The placement personnel must keep themselves in touch with the job opportunities and referral agencies in the community to perform their duties efficiently. The following are some of the characteristics of job placement services.

(a) ***Placement activities should be well-coordinated*:** The job placement services should be well-coordinated to avoid unnecessary duplication of services. The teacher, employer, community agency and job placement personnel should occasionally hold meetings to discuss the problems of job placement. Job placement consists of the following phases:

(i) Orientation to occupational fields. This step introduces the individual to job families requiring similar aptitudes, interest abilities and preparation.

(ii) Relating self to occupational life. This step involves learning about one's own aptitudes and interests and how they are related to a given occupational area. The individual is made available the information about a wide range of occupations. Both group and individual methods may be used in carrying out this phase.

(iii) Choosing an occupational area. The individual is aided to match his abilities with the requirement of an occupation and assisted to choose an occupation suiting to his abilities and interests.

(iv) Job placement. After completing all the above stages of placement services, the next steps are evaluating choices, confirming relationships of personal aptitudes and interests to occupational requirements, locating job opportunities, and referral to potential employers, directly or through cooperating agencies.

(v) Follow-up. This is the last step which determines the appropriateness of his choice.

(b) ***Publicising the placement services:*** The students could be given information related to educational and vocational opportunities. Placement services may be publicized through handbooks, school newspapers, teaching in the class and career conferences, information corner, use of audio-visual aids and meetings with employers etc.

(c) ***Co-operation with community agency:*** If placement services are to be made effective and successful then it is essential to enlist the cooperation of various community agencies.

(d) ***Providing reliable job information:*** The school should provide reliable job information to the students.

(e) ***Using information about pupils:*** The placement service should rely on the information collected in school after collecting reliable data about students.

(f) ***Providing counselling services:*** Regular counselling should be given to those who need it. It may be organised on individual basis or on group basis.

Organisation and Administration of Placement Services

Efficient organisation of placement services depends on the attitude and willingness of the Principal of the school. If the Principal is convinced of the utility of placement services and realizes their importance in the total educational programme and if prepared to meet the expenses, then the programme can be successfully organised. The Principal should decide questions about the needs, facilities, occupation, areas of services, participation of teachers and counsellors, type of clients, and ratio of placement services workers to pupils. The placement services will be most satisfactory if the following principles are kept in view.

(i) Organization should be in harmony with existing school orgniasation.
(ii) Functions of the service should be predetermined.
(iii) The service objectives and policies should be in harmony with the purpose and training objectives of the school.
(iv) An advisory committee of administrators, teachers, counsellors and placement workers should be formed to recommend policies on:
 (a) objective, (b) clearance of information, (c) research activities, (d) follow-up and evaluation.
(v) Duties of the placement workers should be clearly specified. The major duties of placement workers are to,

(a) select placement personnel,
(b) serve as liaison between the school and the employers,
(c) interpret the school programme to the employer,
(d) advise school on the needs for curriculum revision,
(e) coordinate placement services with the other agencies,
(f) conduct field visits,
(h) contribute towards a programme of follow-up,

Follow-up

This is the last step in guidance, services which determines the appropriateness of occupational and educational adjustment of the pupils.

Follow-up is an important aspect of guidance service. Without proper follow-up guidance services are meaningless. It means continuously to evaluate the progress and adjustment of the individuals after giving them counselling regarding courses or vocation. Follow-up may be classified into the following types:

(a) ***Incidental follow-up*:** This type of follow-up is carried on by teachers and counsellors as part of their normal duties. Counsellors and teachers hold interview to get information about the results after counselling and the improvements made by counsellees.

(b) ***Remedial follow-up:*** This type of follow-up is meant for chronic cases which have received intensive remedial help in certain fields. Case histories are prepared and on the basis of the findings, counselling is provided.

(c) ***Systematic follow-up:*** This type of follow-up is to be found where schools have evolved a systematic procedure for following up pupils from one unit of the school to the next higher one.

For example, primary school, junior school, high school or to make the follow-up study of those who have entered the world of work.

(d) ***Follow-up for school leavers:*** This type of follow-up is meant for school and college leaving pupils. The school follows up the pupils after they complete their education. They are aided to get adjusted in their post-school environment.

Functions of Follow-up Services

The concept of follow-up as a service suggests the need for maintaining continuous contacts with students who complete their education and with drop-outs in order to collect useful information, to improve school programmes and to meet the needs and aspirations of the students in a changing society. In our country follow-up services hardly exist except in some professional institutions. The schools, colleges, and universities should seriously think of introducing follow-up services to reduce the problems of the coming generations of students. The follow-up services perform the following functions.

Service Function

(a) Keep in touch with all school, college and university students for years to aid them in making adjustments.

(b) Keep the institution informed of the difficulties former students encounter on jobs or in other institutions.

(c) Locate and offer assistance to unemployed, discouraged or those students who dislike their work.

(d) Improve co-operation between high school and college.

(e) Locate occupational opportunities and keep the school in touch with current occupational trends, requirements and opportunities.

Guidance Functions

(i) Collect and supply teachers, counsellors and administrators information about the problems of former students.

(ii) Supply the information on the demands of different occupations. Information on the skills needed by workers for available jobs provides a basis for modifying the school's occupational training programmes.

Curriculum Research and Revision Function

(i) Evaluate the effectiveness of the school curriculum to modify or expand in the light of the experiences of school leavers.

(ii) Assist in adapting the school programme to the needs of the pupils and the community.

(iii) Evaluate specific portions of the school programme such as guidance services, instruction etc.

(iv) Provide information for pupils and teachers to aid in understanding the school's aims and achievements.

Purposes of Follow-up Surveys

(i) To obtain information as to how well students do after completing their education in vocational, educational and social adjustment.

(ii) To help students realize the problems that lie before them.

(iii) To gain an appraisal of school programmes and services.

(iv) To obtain ideas for improving school services.

(v) The last purpose of the follow-up of school leavers is to gather information of general interest concerning those who have left Such follow-up studies are intended to help all social agencies, including schools to deal with the problems of youth more intelligently.

Procedures in Follow-up Studies

Before initiating follow-up studies, the guidance worker or researchers should keep the following points in view.

(i) The purpose of the study should be specifically detailed out. There should be no ambiguity left as regards the objectives and the type of data to be obtained for the study

(ii) The uses of such data should be specified in the beginning and also the instrument to be used for data collection should be carefully selected, keeping in view the objectives of the studies.

(iii) The researchers should decide the method of processing the data and method of reporting the findings to the appropriate agency. Generally, two main procedures are used in gathering information in follow-up studies, survey through questionnaires and interviews. Both procedures have certain limitations which are very difficult to overcome. One of the limitations of questionnaires which has been reported by all researchers is that the half of those whom questionnaires are sent do not return them. This creates sampling problems. Expert suggests that "to detect certain kind of bias, such as lesser cooperation from persons who failed to make satisfactory adult adjustments, it may be necessary to interview a random sampling of non-respondents and compare findings with those already secured from respondents". Interviews are time-consuming, costly and seldom practicable in the case of individuals who have left the community.

In both questionnaires and interviews, the replies to questions of opinion about the values of training received in school may be somewhat too favourable. Everyone tends to remember pleasant experiences and to forget the unpleasant ones. When one has been out of school a few years, his memory of school life tends to be coloured by sentiment and he is liable to exaggerate the values derived from the school programme.

A representative sample of each group is interviewed in order to obtain more extensive and detailed information that can be included in a questionnaire.

Responsibility for making follow-up studies is decentralized so that each class is advised to follow up his own class as they leave school.

The adviser's analysis of the data is made available to other school functionaries and is combined with those of other advisers in order to give a complete picture for the school system.

Conclusions concerning causal relationships are drawn with caution.

Characteristics of Follow-up Plan

Traxler in his book Techniques of Guidance has given the following salient characteristics of a follow-up plan.

(i) It is planned to serve the needs of both the individual and the school.
(ii) It begins before the students leave school.
(iii) It is continuous.
(iv) It includes all school leavers.
(v) Each class is followed up for at least five years.
(vi) Procedures are used to ensure the return of questionnaires from 80 per cent of those to whom these are sent.
(vii) The significant items for each individual's return are transferred to his cumulative record card.
(viii) The follow-up plan is coordinated with a post-school counselling service.
(ix) So far as possible, the cooperation of lay citizens is obtained in collecting, studying and using the follow-up data.

Planning better Follow-up Studies

Follow-up studies are very important to evaluate the outcome of schools. In our country, very few studies have been conducted on educational and vocational follow-ups. Everyone feels that follow-up studies are very valuable to improve the existing programmes. To attain greater value and to justify time and money required to be spent; follow-up studies should be conducted following a scientific procedure which is given here.

(i) Follow-up studies be carried to their logical conclusion: Generally a follow-up is conducted in three phases — (*a*) The first phase involves the systematic collection of data from former students using standardized or self-made tools. (*b*) The second phase involves the analysis and interpretation of the information collected and the results of the study should be presented to all persons involved in the study. (*c*) The third phase is important because it is concerned with planned modifications in the educational programme on the basis of the findings of the study.

(ii) Follow-up studies be conducted at regular intervals: If schools are really interested in improving their curricular programmes in accordance with the fast-changing socio-economic conditions then it becomes imperative to conduct follow-up studies at regular intervals. The interval may be of two, three or five years which may be decided keeping into consideration the resources of the school.

(iii) Follow-up study be school projected, not one-man projected: Follow-up study should be taken up by a team of teachers and students and if possible some interested persons from the local community may also be involved in the study.

(iv) Follow-up study results must be handled effectively: This is an important step in the follow-up study. If the findings and conclusions of the study are not effectively reported and publicised among the members then it can nullify the great deal of effort spent in gathering facts. Better methods of reporting data to professional and lay groups need to be developed in order to gain their understanding and support.

(v) Technical aspects of conducting follow-up studies deserves greater attention: This is the last step which deserves special attention of the experts. This deals with the technical aspects of tools to be used for data collection. Tools to be used should be objective and reliable.

Index